# BANKING
# ON
# CONFIDENCE

# BANKING ON CONFIDENCE

## A GUIDEBOOK TO FINANCIAL LITERACY

### DALE K. CLINE

**Research and Writing Assistance by Tina R. Lineberger, CPA**

BANKING ON CONFIDENCE
A GUIDEBOOK TO FINANCIAL LITERACY

iUniverse books may be ordered through booksellers or by contacting:

iUniverse
1663 Liberty Drive
Bloomington, IN 47403
www.iuniverse.com
1-800-Authors (1-800-288-4677)

ISBN: 978-1-4917-5582-2 (sc)
ISBN: 978-1-4917-5839-7 (hc)
ISBN: 978-1-4917-5583-9 (e)

Library of Congress Control Number: 2014922504

Print information available on the last page.

iUniverse rev. date: 12/11/2015

**In memory of**
**Oren L. Cline**
**Father, mentor, best friend**

# CONTENTS

# INTRODUCTION

*In our time, the curse is monetary illiteracy, just as inability*

*to read plain print was the curse of earlier centuries.*

—*Ezra Pound*[1]

The above quote from American poet and intellectual Ezra Pound sums up the inspiration behind this book, which was born out of frustration with the myriad conflicting stories, reports, and debates about the economy. Regardless of our stations in life, we are all affected by the economy at the local, national, and even global levels. And when we encounter so much contradictory information, we are left wondering just how it all really works.

The average citizen has a difficult time overcoming monetary illiteracy. Although a wealth of information is available from books and media outlets, much of it is laced with political sentiment. Separating the wheat from the chaff, so to speak, is difficult.

This book is not a full economics course by any means. It is meant solely to offer the average citizen a fundamental understanding of the economic world in which we live and work from an everyday point of view. It is for anyone and everyone who is optimistic, pessimistic, or just curious about the way the economy actually operates. It is written to be user friendly. There are some nuts and bolts about how the banking system works and how the money supply expands and contracts. Since economics is really concerned with how people think about and behave with their money, it's mostly common sense.

This is not an investment guide, though there is discussion of how to consider values as they relate to wealth creation. It is not a political discourse, but there are references to the role that the government plays in economic policy. Global matters are presented within a framework that the average reader will grasp, with explanations that apply economic concepts to daily life. Historical events, such as the relatively recent "Great Recession," are interwoven throughout the text to provide real-world examples of economic outcomes. While the illustrations used may relate to a specific time in history, the lessons to be gained are timeless. Ideally, readers will be armed with new insight into the way the economy actually works, through both discussion and examples, thereby empowering them to make better decisions for themselves and their families.

Economics is often referred to as "the dismal science."[2] That description, coined by Scotsman Thomas Carlyle in the nineteenth century, was inspired by the theory of economist Thomas Malthus, which proposed that human population growth would perpetually outpace the availability of natural resources, resulting in a general state of inescapable misery. That does paint quite a bleak and dismal picture. Even now, in modern times, the economic reports that garner the most attention are those warning of some negative outcome. The general outlook is pessimistic, casting a negative pallor on the study of economics.

The current generation of college students has come of age in a time of economic uncertainty, with reports of recession and unemployment the norm. Even older Americans have become accustomed to the political mistrust and gridlock that seems to be commonplace. Perhaps that has colored the perspectives of many Americans who view the economy with skepticism. Could that lack of trust offer some explanation for why so many remain vague in their economic understanding? Possibly, although the more likely reason is that the economy seems unwieldy and complicated. With its many moving parts and labels, it is intimidating for someone who is not well versed in economic terminology. Yet it actually is quite understandable, and far from dismal, when explained in everyday language.

Let's be honest: most people do not find economics to be stimulating or exciting. *Complicated* and *mundane* are adjectives more likely to come to mind. It is my hope that this book changes that outlook. Realizing that we can understand how the economy is likely to be affected by certain events or conditions and use that information to determine the appropriate course of action to take for our own economic security can empower us, and that is exciting. The goal of this endeavor is to improve monetary literacy for those of us who care about the economy, increase our knowledge base, and inspire us with confidence in our own understanding, one chapter at a time. Let us begin.

# PART ONE

## HOW THE ECONOMY WORKS: NUTS AND BOLTS

Leonardo da Vinci once said, "The noblest pleasure is the joy of understanding." It is with the goal of gaining greater understanding that we venture into the world of economics. As if we were painting a landscape, we will begin with the basic framework and then add subject matter one layer at a time, gradually building in the foreground, the horizon, the sky, and all the other details that complete the picture.

The economy is ever changing. If economic outcomes were completely predictable, it would be simple for economists to develop prescribed formulas to handle any situation. Because the economy is a function of human circumstances, there are no universal formulas to provide systematic solutions for each and every scenario that comes about. So any study of the economy must consider the actions of people. That certainly adds a layer of unpredictability!

As with politics, we all have different experiences and outlooks that color the way we view the economy. But the universal truths remain constant. There are basic facts that apply to any study of the economy, and these facts provide the foundation upon which the following chapters are built. Adding individual interpretation to the facts allows each of us to apply our understanding in our daily decision making. While we might each see things a bit differently, if we understand the universal truths, we will make better decisions.

This will not be an arduous journey. The chapters are presented in a way that will gradually introduce topics and provide background without belaboring the point. Think of it as a stroll down a meandering road. We will stop off at a few points along the way. We may spend more time at certain stops than at others, and we will see new things as we go. But when we reach our destination, we will have gained new understanding. Hopefully, we will have enjoyed the scenery along the way as well.

# CHAPTER 1

## CONFIDENCE, MONETARY POLICY, AND FISCAL POLICY: THE THREE PILLARS

Imagine that the economy sits upon three pillars: confidence, monetary policy, and fiscal policy. Those are probably not the first terms that come to mind when you think about economics, but they are essential components of real economic understanding. A healthy economy cannot exist without these three pillars operating in equilibrium. Each plays an individual role, but all of them must be present and working together to optimize economic growth. Supply and demand, productivity, innovation, exponential technology, and any other of the more familiar economic terms all rest upon the foundation of these three pillars.

### CONFIDENCE

Of the three pillars, the most important is confidence. Such a simple word, yet it may be the most important ingredient for a nation's economic well-being. The other two elements cannot compensate for a lack of confidence. Without it, the economy cannot prosper.

Why is confidence so important? It sets the tone for everything else, infusing a positive spirit that inspires the ability to overcome seemingly insurmountable odds. If you don't believe that this country can recover from a disaster, consider the response of the United States after the December 7, 1941, Japanese attack on Pearl Harbor, which marked the beginning of US involvement in World War II. With the fate of our entire nation at stake, and facing a dark and desperate future, we knew we had to win that war. There was simply no other option. With confidence derived from the fear and fury of war, we did win, but in doing so we cast normal and ordinary monetary policy and fiscal policy to the wind. At that desperate time, there could be no concern about maintaining economic equilibrium. We did what we had to do as a nation, both private sector and government, to win the war.

Consequently, by the end of World War II, the government owed more than it ever had in its history relative to the annual economy. The nation, having financed the massive cost of war but now fueled by victory and optimism for a brighter future, reduced that massive indebtedness within less than a decade through rapid growth in the private economy. Confidence inspires people to imagine a greater future and to learn and use new technology to create a better world. Without confidence, we really haven't much else. It is that simple.

## MONETARY POLICY

The second pillar, monetary policy, is the process of adjusting, on an ongoing basis, the supply of money in the economy, the availability of credit, and the cost of borrowing. The implementation of monetary policy falls under the authority of the Federal Reserve Bank. The Fed monitors a myriad of economic indicators and data that decision makers use to determine the actions necessary to maintain the appropriate amount of money in the economy to meet its end objectives of relatively full employment and low inflation.

Working directly with the banking system, the Fed plays a key role in the way the modern monetary system operates. Depending on its goals, the Fed will implement actions that encourage expansion of credit in an attempt to stimulate economic activity, or it may discourage borrowing, thereby slowing growth. Hopefully, decision makers will achieve their goals most of the time, although it can be as much art as science.

Using a variety of available tools, Fed authorities constantly seek to create the perfect balance in the economy to allow it to thrive. It's a bit like the search for the perfect porridge in the fairy tale of the three bears seeking the bowl that is "not too hot, not too cold, but just right." What is "just right" in one set of circumstances may spell disaster in another.

With so many moving parts and an ever-changing fiscal environment, there is no single prescription to cure a particular economic ill. Monetary policy experts are constantly forecasting and attempting to make the most accurate predictions possible, as their decisions are the ones most likely to affect the economic lives of individuals. They carry a huge burden. Still, the obligation to get it right is not theirs alone, as monetary policy is permanently interwoven with fiscal policy. They must be perfectly synchronized.

## FISCAL POLICY

Fiscal policy, the final pillar, is all about the government. The goal of fiscal policy is to control government spending levels and set tax rates in a proper balance in order to serve the private economy. It is probably the most well known but least understood of the three pillars.

Because it is carried out by way of the body of laws established by Congress, fiscal policy is often referenced in headlines and sound bites. Taxes are of particular interest because of their direct effect on each of us. Simply stated, taxation is the government's primary method of revenue collection. Fiscal policy seeks to balance that revenue with government spending and other regulations in a way that allows the private sector to flourish.

Think of it as a toolkit. By adjusting tax revenues or budgetary spending, the government has the ability to implement changes directed at influencing and balancing aggregate demand, inflation, and gross domestic product (GDP). Historically, the portion of the private economy paid into the government through taxation was approximately 18 to 20 percent. In more recent years, that percentage has been on an upward trajectory, meaning the government continues to take an ever bigger slice of the private economy.

Many believe that amount to be excessive because the

revenue being funneled into a government program is no longer available to stimulate the private economy. Others believe that large government programs make such a great contribution to the well-being of the citizens that paying higher taxes is a justified way to spread the wealth. Government spending does pour money into the private economy when it is being used to purchase goods and services for government projects, and there are theories that suggest that deficit spending is a worthwhile stimulus for a sluggish economy.

While there are differing economic theories and opposing viewpoints, all agree that fiscal policy does have an impact on the health of the economy, and it is clear that, to maximize its effectiveness, it must be executed in concert with monetary policy. Some argue that the role of monetary policy should be secondary to that of fiscal policy, while others maintain that when it comes to government regulation, less is more. Many believe that the government should provide a regulatory framework and then step out of the way, allowing the economy to thrive without the suppression of excessive governmental bureaucracy. Regardless of political leanings, all would agree that the government is obligated to carry out the mandate of the US Constitution and, in so doing, create a balanced playing field and protect the property rights and personal freedoms that make America such a great country.

## GDP

The previous discussion referenced the term *GDP*, an acronym for gross domestic product. It is frequently used in economic discussions, but many people don't really understand what it means. Why do we monitor GDP? How is it calculated? And why is it considered one of the most important measures of the economy's health and citizens' standard of living?

In a nutshell, GDP is the market value of all officially recognized final goods and services produced within a country in a given time period. The word *final*, as used here, means that the value of a given good or service that is produced is counted at the point of completion of the good or service, and the various components and wages are included within that final value. In other words, although a car might be comprised of metal, glass, tires, etc., the individual parts—for example, the windshield or tires—are only included once in the GDP as part of the final production value of the car. If they were sold separately, as when you purchase a new set of tires for your car, they would be counted because they are being sold for final use.

Although there are several methods for calculating GDP, in principal, each method produces approximately the same result. Understanding GDP is critical to most any discussion of the economy because it measures, in the broadest sense, our economic health as a nation. Is the economy growing at a reasonable rate to provide relatively full employment for those able to work? Are we earning a gradual and continuously improving standard of living as a nation? Is the final GDP calculation for a given year the *real* growth of the nation, or is it being expressed in current prices at current dollar values, also referred to as *nominal GDP*, without an adjustment for inflation? Are we expanding our economy at a rate that retains or improves our strength relative to the rest of the world? All of these questions hinge on a basic understanding of GDP and its role in measuring the economy.

## BALANCE

Thinking again about the image of three pillars, strong and yet flexible, we get a sense of the balance that is necessary for the economy to operate like a well-oiled machine. In a perfect world, these three supports would function in easy harmony, fluctuating as necessary to maintain a strong system in which the economy could flourish. But the world doesn't always work that way. With so many moving parts in our economy, we would be foolish to expect to maintain perfect harmony. The goal is balance, and as we know, confidence is the key.

With decisions regarding monetary policy and fiscal policy being made within the political arena, confidence can be elusive. Politicians debate and legislate and sometimes seem to accomplish nothing more than gridlock. The resulting public frustration leads to a lack of confidence in those decision makers, and that can translate into fear for our economic future. Our democracy allows us the privilege of choosing our leaders, and administrations inevitably change from one election cycle to another. The shifts in ideology can swing the pendulum back and forth, with fiscal policies changing in response. A properly functioning economy requires monetary policies and fiscal policies that work in harmony toward a common goal. Policies may change, but ideally, the goal should remain steadfast. Through it all, confidence must remain or the balance will falter and the economy cannot thrive.

So with balance in mind, let's revisit the question we touched on in the discussion of fiscal policy. What is the proper balance between the public and private sectors? This tug of war is often the root of political polarization, thrusting the debate regarding the balance of power and money between the government and the people into the heart of many fiscal policy decisions. It is an age-old question, the answer to which plays a pivotal role in fostering confidence in our leaders and, thus, our economic future.

Is there a point of equilibrium that maintains a necessary amount of government activity while fostering growth in the private sector and, therefore, a healthy overall economy? In the political arena, we generally hear such buzzwords as *bigger government* and *deficit spending* with a negative connotation. While most Americans do not understand all of the inner workings of the banking system or the money supply, the average citizen does understand income taxes and the impact on his or her wallet. Yet it is really all part of the same interplay between monetary and fiscal policy.

Consider the following example: If a relatively well-to-do American citizen is earning $200,000 per year at a 20 percent tax rate (with that 20 percent as an example of a rate close to the overall percentage of government revenue to GDP, historically), then he or she would pay around $40,000 per year in taxes, resulting in $160,000 of discretionary income. Now assume that he spends $100,000 on his family for daily living expenses—things such as food, housing, and transportation—and also for educating his children, hopefully in fine colleges. The remaining $60,000 is now available for additional consumption or savings and investments.

If we assume that he is thinking about the future of his family, including his children and grandchildren, we can imagine that he will invest in innovative things that he believes will be valuable in the future and will, thus, pay him back through dividends and capital gains. As that $60,000 comes out of his pocket, it goes into fueling economic growth by financing successful existing companies or innovative new companies, which in turn will invest that capital in new facilities, new technology, new employees, and newer and more efficient products. The economy is better off, and our investor will hopefully be rewarded with dividends and value growth on his invested money.

Now assume that instead of a 20 percent tax rate, our citizen pays taxes at a rate of 30 percent. An additional $20,000 of his income will go to the government, and he will only have $40,000 available for investment. The government now has an extra $20,000 to spend on public services, entitlement programs, defense, domestic and foreign aid, and all of its other functions. Is the country as a whole better off financing these government programs or putting that money to work in the private sector, which is generally seen as the engine that drives the economy? Some believe that when we allocate funds to the public sector, it eliminates the opportunity for that money to be used to fuel economic growth. They argue that the government is *crowding out* the private sector.

Aside from the impact of a larger government on the economy as a whole, the funds injected into the government are used to finance bureaucratic jobs and federal programs, which some believe are acting to over-regulate the economy. In some cases, the workers who fill government jobs could perhaps be better employed, for themselves and the economy, in the private sector. So when we speak of the government crowding out the private sector, we are talking about more than an increase in government borrowing and spending. While these are economic questions, there are strong political undercurrents that complicate the issue and sometimes create anger or fear instead of confidence and inspiration.

Are lower taxes and less government always better for the private sector? What if the government only funneled its expenditures into productive programs and infrastructure? Is the $20,000 from our example better utilized by the government to carry out its functions or invested in the private sector, the driver of the economy? Which produces the better result for the citizen and for the country? Of course, this can—and often does—become the center point of political debate. While it may be compelling, it is not within the context of this book to make those arguments. This is a discussion of economic understanding, and in that spirit, we will disregard political leanings and focus on gaining understanding of the way the economy works.

Think about how far the United States has come in just a couple hundred years. For such a young nation, the growth and innovation are simply astounding. The US Constitution provides a strong framework, but the many rulings and laws that have been implemented throughout our history have created a complicated and tangled regulatory framework within which the economy must function. The key, as we know, is balance. And balance can be difficult to maintain when the three pillars are being tugged in different directions.

In some ways, the world's largest economy is a fragile giant. The larger it grows, the more difficult it becomes to alter its course when things begin to tilt out of balance. Fiscal policies change from one administration to another, with monetary policies adapting in order to maintain equilibrium. That is the nature of our government, and viewed with historical perspective, it works pretty well. Policies aside, however, we can see that the most robust times were also the times when confidence was high. As time marches forward, we can only learn from past mistakes and hope to recognize obstacles when they arise, attempting to maintain balance and confidence in our future.

# CHAPTER 2

## BASIC ACCOUNTING AND FINANCIAL STATEMENTS

Accounting is a very old profession...

It is also the basis for understanding what makes the economy tick. It provides the framework that allows each and every economic transaction to be expressed in a systematic way. While much of the more complex accounting rules and regulations are beyond what the average person would wish to grasp, a basic understanding of the system is essential to understanding how the economy works. It operates like a truth serum, separating fact from fiction. If a particular theory cannot be proven through accounting, then its validity is in question. If a transaction cannot be expressed through an accounting entry, something is amiss.

Accounting, as we know it today, is based on a system called double-entry bookkeeping, which was first codified in the fifteenth century by a Franciscan friar named Luca Pacioli. While merchants and governments had been recording transactions in similar ways prior to this time, it was Pacioli who first described the system and, thereby, outlined the means by which all who used it should operate. It consisted of structured methods of entering transactions into journals and ledgers using debits and credits to affect the appropriate accounts. The system remains largely the same today, although there are myriad rules and regulations that serve to ensure consistency from one set of books to another.

## ECONOMIC INSIGHT

Accounting is the bedrock, or foundation, of the economy. It enables us to record all monetary transactions in such a way that we can measure our *assets* (what we have), our *liabilities* (what we owe), and the difference between those, which is our *capital* (wealth or net worth). We also record income and expenses with this system, which allows us to determine profit or loss for a particular period being measured. At its simplest, accounting allows us to understand the particulars of an individual's or company's financial position. However, we can use the same language to understand the broader economy. Accounting is essentially a doorway to economic insight, as it allows us to translate any set of financial data into a format that can be more easily compared, contrasted, and analyzed. That common format lends confidence to our ability to rely on the data for economic decision making.

Perhaps most important for a study of economics is that accounting allows us to understand the way the modern banking system works. Believe it or not, journal entries tell the whole story. Because banking is the heartbeat of the economy, it is crucial to understand the role that banks play in the creation of money. Accounting provides us with the tools for that understanding. So while it may seem bland or mechanical, accounting can open our eyes to the way the economy really works.

A user who is looking at an entity's financial statements or records—whether that entity is a business, a government agency, or an individual—should be able to understand them with relative ease because they were prepared using universal principles. The application of the rules and regulations has matured along with the oversight that promulgates the accounting profession today. That oversight sends a message of confidence to users of financial data, as it ensures uniformity of reporting. Consistently ranked among the most respected professions, accounting is typically viewed as being steady and somewhat safe. While the profession may not be perceived as glamorous, the principles and regulations that are its hallmarks provide a framework for understanding how the economy works.

## DEBITS AND CREDITS

It all begins with debits and credits. Each recording, or entry, that is made in our *books*—the common term used to refer to journals or ledgers—is entered in such a way that two different accounts are affected, debiting one account and crediting another, to fully describe the transaction. The debits are recorded on the left-side column in a journal and the credits are recorded on the right. The total debits must equal the total credits, thus providing a way to ensure that transactions are *in balance*. As long as the proper types of accounts are debited and credited, then net worth (assets minus liabilities) can be properly determined.

Asset and expense accounts are considered *debit accounts.* Debiting these accounts increases them. Liabilities, revenue, and capital accounts are considered credit accounts. Crediting these accounts increases them. Some simple examples follow.

Assume this is the first year of operation for Generic Manufacturing Company. If Generic sells a product for $100 in a cash transaction, the correct entry is:

|  | DEBITS | CREDITS |
| --- | --- | --- |
| Cash (asset account) | $100 | |
| Sales (revenue account) | | $100 |

If Generic pays cash wages of $50, the correct entry is:

|  | DEBITS | CREDITS |
| --- | --- | --- |
| Wages (expense account) | $50 | |
| Cash (asset account) | | $50 |

In the first example, the entry debiting the cash (asset) account and crediting revenue reflects the impact of the receipt of cash upon the sale of a product. Payment of an expense, as in the second example, is evidenced by debiting (increasing) the expense account and crediting cash, the asset, to reflect the expenditure.

When entering these transactions into a journal, the first step in the creation of accounting records, the debits are entered in the column on the left side and the credits on the right. In our examples, cash comes into the checking account when the sale is recognized, therefore we debit cash and credit sales. Wages are paid from the cash account and recorded as expenses, so we debit wages and credit cash.

The activity for each account is maintained in the journal, but it can also be expressed using a *T-Account*. Called such because it looks like a capital letter *T*, a T-account is a tool that accountants have long used to quickly and easily keep up with transactions. This is just an alternative method of reflecting a transaction. While it is not necessary to use T-accounts, they can help users visualize the entries. Some accountants prefer journal entries, while others use T-accounts for simplicity. Computerized bookkeeping typically operates in a journal format, essentially eliminating the need for T-accounts, but many accountants still prefer them when working out the proper accounting for proposed transactions or attempting to track adjustments to particular accounts. They may appear old-fashioned, but they still work.

These are the T-Accounts for the previous examples:

|  | Cash (Asset) | | Wages (Expense) | | Sales (Revenue) | |
|---|---|---|---|---|---|---|
| ENTRY #1 | $100 | | | | | $100 |
| ENTRY #2 | | $50 | $50 | | | |

After these two transactions, the company has $50 in cash ($100 sales revenue less $50 paid for wages). When looking back at either the journal entries or the T-accounts, we can see that the company has recognized revenue of $100 and expenses of $50, thereby producing a $50 profit. All obligations have been paid, so there are no liabilities. Since we know that net worth, or capital, is total assets less total liabilities, we can see that Generic's net worth is $50, which is the total of the assets ($50 cash) minus the total liabilities ($0).

Notice that the debits are on the left of each column, the credits are on the right, and the total of the debits equals the total of the credits. Possibly the most basic of accounting principles, this is a truth that applies to every single transaction that is recorded. Regardless of the method used, total debits should equal total credits. Aging accountants sometimes tease each other, saying, "Hey, buddy, don't forget that the debits are on the left!"

Having established that all transactions are recorded with this common format of debits and credits, we can take a look at several different types of entries. Cash transactions, such as those in our example for Generic Manufacturing Company, are usually the simplest entries. Other transactions may not involve any cash outlay or current income recognition at all. They may record a timing difference, such as a liability incurred for later payment of cash or a receivable from customer credit sales booked before cash payments are actually received.

For example, if Generic Manufacturing decides to borrow money from a bank, the cash received is not income; it is simply money being borrowed now that will be repaid later. The company would record the loan by debiting cash and crediting a "loan payable" account. Although this entry does not affect company income or expenses, it is important in recording the borrowing activity and accounting for the cash being deposited now and repaid later, along with any interest expense incurred. Essentially, every financial transaction that occurs for a company, plus some noncash tax-related ones, must be recorded on the books in order to accurately reflect the company's financial position. Typically, many types of transactions will be booked during a reporting period, which may be any stated length of time but is typically no longer than one year for most businesses.

The ultimate goal for all of this accounting is to produce a set of financial statements—typically including but not limited an *Income Statement* (sometimes called a Profit & Loss Statement or abbreviated as P&L) and a *Balance Sheet* (sometimes referred to as a Statement of Financial Position or abbreviated as BS)—that provides users with a picture of the company's overall financial position as of the end of its reporting period. The following is an example of a basic Income Statement:

ABC Company
Income Statement

|  | Debits | Credits |
|---|---|---|
| Revenue: | | |
| Sales | | $100,000 |
| | | |
| Expenses: | | |
| Wages | $50,000 | |
| Material | 20,000 | |
| Overhead | 10,000 | |
| | | |
| Profit | | $20,000 |

and a basic Balance Sheet:

ABC Company
Balance Sheet

|  | Debits | Credits |
|---|---|---|
| Assets |  |  |
| Cash | $20,000 |  |
|  |  |  |
| Liabilities & Capital |  |  |
| Liabilities |  | $0 |
| Capital (Retained Earnings/Profits) |  | 20,000 |

These simple examples tell us that ABC Company started on Day 1 with nothing and ended with $20,000 in its bank account, which represents all of its capital (i.e., profits). The Income Statement covers activity for a certain reporting period, and the Balance Sheet covers the financial position at a stated point in time in the life of the business.

Considering that the balances on the balance sheet on the last day of an accounting period are still there on the first day of the next, it is easy to see that at the beginning of Day 1 of the second year, the Income Statement will start with zero transactions (because there hasn't been any activity yet) and the Balance Sheet will begin with $20,000 cash and $20,000 in capital. This recognizes that the profit or loss of each period is "zeroed out" on the Income Statement and moved into the capital account on the Balance Sheet, allowing profit or loss for the new period to start over at zero.

The preceding discussion describes, in the simplest of ways, how a business—part of the private sector of the economy—accounts for its transactions. Although the public sector, or government, operates under the same accounting principles and the double-entry bookkeeping system, reporting is handled a bit differently. Accounting for private-sector businesses focuses on reporting financial activity and, often, disclosing financial position for purposes of budgetary planning or shareholder reporting. For a governmental entity, where there is no profit motive, fiscal accountability is at the core of the reporting requirements. While budgeting may be a consideration, the primary focus is on compliance and disclosure. The entity is under an obligation to report its handling of public resources in its efforts to accomplish stated objectives. From a reader's standpoint, the financial statements will appear quite similar. Often referred to as *fund accounting*, governmental accounting revolves around the cash flows related to the entity or project in question. Typically, in lieu of a capital or earnings account, the balance sheet will reflect a net fund balance.

So far, we have viewed a simple company and the illustrations of its accounting entries and reports, but we haven't talked about the driver of this private-sector company—which, at its heart, is the commercial banking system. Without banks to supply money in the form of credit to the economy, this company would operate much differently. Without money and credit, we would return to a barter system, whereby citizens traded goods and services. That's the way the world worked prior to the evolution of the banking industry and the implementation of accounting principles.

## ACCOUNTING IN THE BANKING INDUSTRY

Before we delve into how money is created and supplied into the economy, we need to examine the way the banking industry accounts for transactions and how that accounting system is reflected on financial statements. Though the accounting principles remain the same as for general businesses and banks, their respective roles in the economy are quite different. When we think of a business, we think of things like a company making and selling shoes, a restaurant selling hamburgers, a developer producing and selling computer software, a doctor providing healthcare to us, a homebuilder building our home, or a barber giving a haircut. A bank, on the other hand, enables all of us, in our respective businesses, to literally *do* business. Besides processing our transactions and maintaining our deposits, it lends money to borrowers.

A typical bank's financial statements might look something like the following:

USA Bank
Income Statement

|  | Expenses (Debits) | Revenues (Credits) |
|---|---|---|
| Income: |  |  |
| Interest Income |  | $200,000 |
| Expenses: |  |  |
| Wages paid to employees | $50,000 |  |
| Interest paid to depositors | 50,000 |  |
| Other overhead | 50,000 |  |
| Total Expenses | 150,000 |  |
| Profit (credit) or Loss (debit) |  | $50,000 |

And, hypothetically:

USA Bank
Balance Sheet

|  | Debits | Credits |
|---|---|---|
| Assets |  |  |
| Loans to Borrowers | $1,000,000 |  |
| Government Bonds | 1,000,000 |  |
| Liabilities & Capital |  |  |
| Deposits from Customers |  | $1,800,000 |
| Capital |  | 200,000 |
| Totals | $2,000,000 | $2,000,000 |

The point to remember is that, while the financial statements for a typical manufacturing or service business might look somewhat different from those of a bank, they both are based on the same basic accounting principles. Assets = Liabilities + Capital, always!

The goal of this discussion of accounting and financial statements is not to build a full working knowledge of accounting, but to lay the groundwork, the platform, to allow us to move into a discussion of how money is created and passed into the economy. Accounting truly is the language of business. More than just debits and credits, it is the common foundation that allows for the communication of useful, relevant, and reliable financial information. As such, when we look at the way the banking system works within the economy, we will rely on none other than basic accounting principles to understand where our money comes from.

# CHAPTER 3

## RELATIONSHIP OF THE FEDERAL RESERVE BANK AND THE US TREASURY DEPARTMENT

One evening not long ago, over dinner, I asked my wife, "Dear, do you know what the US Department of the Treasury and the Federal Reserve Bank actually do—what their respective roles are in the US economy?"

She gazed downward and quietly, almost apologetically, answered, "No."

Don't you think we have great conversation in my house? I'm kidding. I just laughed and said to her, "It wasn't meant to be a serious question, and most others don't know either."

I've learned that most people really don't know. They're busy with their lives or maybe just don't care. And that's okay—we all do what we do. I suspect most of you reading this already know quite a bit and you obviously want to learn more. The truth is that, for those who want to gain a real understanding of the way the economy works, a basic knowledge of how the banking system works is a must. And to grasp that, one must be familiar with the Federal Reserve System and the role of the US Treasury.

## THE ROLE OF THE FEDERAL RESERVE

The Federal Reserve, commonly referred to as the Fed, is the central bank, the nation's bank, the bank to the commercial banking system, and the banker of last resort. Created by the Federal Reserve Act in 1913, the system is made up of twelve regional banks and twenty-five branches. Leadership is provided by a seven-member panel known as the board of governors. The members of the Board of Governors are selected from among the officers of the regional banks and are nominated by the president and confirmed by the Senate.

Based in Washington, DC, the board is charged with guiding and administering the activities and policies of the regional reserve banks as well as providing broad oversight of the nation's financial-services industry. Board members are frequently called upon to communicate with Congress and provide updates to governmental leaders in regard to current financial conditions and the overall health of the economy. While these duties are certainly important, perhaps the most critical role that board members fulfill is the interaction with and oversight of the Federal Open Market Committee (FOMC). It is through this arm of the Federal Reserve System that the board is able to implement and carry out its monetary policy, seeking to bring about stable levels of employment and moderate inflation.

Although many believe that the Fed is a governmental

operation, in actuality, it is an independent institution. While its shares are owned by its member banks, it is somewhat akin to a co-op in that ownership of shares is required for membership. Sale or transfer of the shares is restricted, so they cannot be publicly traded, and dividends are paid at a set rate. The Fed's annual earnings are turned over to the Treasury Department so shareholders do not benefit from any net revenues. Because the Fed is not operated for a profit, the shares do not hold an element of investment, and there is no sense of control by or obligation to shareholders, attributing a sense of operational independence.

Additionally, the Fed is able to make decisions and carry out its monetary policies without governmental approval, thereby making it independent of governmental control. However, it is subject to congressional oversight and reporting, and there is always a possibility that Congress could enact statutes that would affect the powers of the Fed. Because the interests of the government and the Fed are so closely linked, the two often act in partnership, making the Fed somewhat of an agent of the government. So while it functions with autonomy, it still operates under the shadow of the government, and each administration does exercise a degree of influence over Fed activities.

## THE US TREASURY DEPARTMENT AND ITS RELATIONSHIP WITH THE FED

The US Department of the Treasury is not an independent entity by any means. It is owned by the citizens of the United States. Created by an act of Congress in 1798, it is the department of the US government that is responsible for managing the nation's money. The Treasury manages our government's accounts, collects tax revenue, oversees issuance of debt, and pays bills. Since it is the money purse, you might say it runs the whole show. The Treasury carries out its many duties through branches that operate under the US Treasury umbrella.

One such branch is the Internal Revenue Service. Think of the IRS as sort of a collection agency for the Treasury. When you send in tax money you owe to the Internal Revenue Service, you're really sending it to the Treasury, where it is used to pay the government's bills. And since the Treasury is charged with collecting revenues and paying bills for the country, it has a vested interest in fostering a stable economy. That's where the Fed comes into play. Working together, the Fed and the Treasury carry out their respective duties to promote economic health. The Treasury manages the government's money, and the Federal Reserve serves as the government's bank, processing transactions on behalf of the Treasury.

Additionally, recall that the Federal Reserve is technically a nonprofit institution, turning its profits over to the government. Between the Fed's profits and the revenues collected by the IRS, most all federally mandated levies end up in the Treasury Department bank accounts at, you guessed it, the Fed. And that's from where the funds are disbursed. Whether for entitlement programs (think Social Security, Medicare, Medicaid, Welfare), national defense, national parks, or other government operations, the Treasury accounts at the Fed are collection central and disbursement central.

## WHERE DOES OUR MONEY COME FROM?

Most people know that the US government authorizes the printing of Federal Reserve notes, or dollars, and the minting of coins. Other than the value of the materials used in the production of the money, it technically has no intrinsic value. We could just as easily be using furs or stones or shells, as in the past. But our system operates based on paper notes and coins that are assigned value based on their denomination.

Since we know that the US Treasury is the arm of the government that manages our nation's money, it stands to reason that the responsibility for production of our money would rest with the Treasury. The US Bureau of Engraving and Printing, one of the departments of the US Treasury, is charged with printing paper money for delivery to the Federal Reserve. Coinage is minted under authority of another Treasury division, the US Mint. Actual production of the currency entails a very complicated process designed to achieve such a level of quality that the notes and coins cannot be easily counterfeited.

The Federal Reserve purchases the cash from the Treasury at a given price, generally based on manufacturing cost in the case of notes and face value for coinage. The notes and coins are carried on the Fed's balance sheet as assets (debits), and payment to the Treasury is made by crediting the Treasury's account at the Fed. The Fed then introduces the notes and coins into the currency supply by selling them to the eight regional Federal Reserve banks at face value. That transaction is reflected as a credit on the Fed's balance sheet and a debit to the banks' reserve accounts. From there it filters into the commercial banks and, eventually, into our pockets. The banks carry the currency on their balance sheets as assets, so when we walk into the bank and withdraw cash from our checking or savings account, the bank credits its asset account and debits our account.

## SEIGNIORAGE

But why is the currency *sold* to the banks, and what about the difference in the amount the Fed pays for the cash and the price at which it sells it to the banks? Who is the beneficiary of that profit? If the Fed pays a few cents for a five- or ten-dollar bill and then sells it to the banking system at face value, there is potential for the Fed to make a tremendous profit. The term for this profitable sale of raw currency from the Fed to the banking system is *seigniorage*, and its value as a practice in our modern economy lies in the fact that our currency is merely an obligation of the government. Simply put, the coins and notes that we know as money are representations of liabilities of our government. They are given value based on what our government promises to honor in exchange for them.

The entire system is based on the fact that the government will only accept US dollars and cents in payment for taxes. So the value cycle begins and ends with the government. The built-in difference in the face value assigned to units of currency over the cost to produce the money results in seigniorage profits that ultimately benefit the Treasury. While the currency is purchased from the Treasury by the Fed in the process previously described, the Fed is simply a mechanism in the supply chain of currency to the economy.

It does not stand alone as a profit-making entity. Any profit from the sale of currency to the banks is returned to the Treasury, along with the interest paid on any Treasury notes held by the Fed. Because these funds return to the Treasury, which is ultimately held by the citizens of the United States, it is the people who eventually benefit in the form of reduced taxes or an offset to government spending.

## BUDGET DEFICITS AND FINANCING GOVERNMENT DEBT

We constantly hear about our growing national debt and deficit spending, but how many of us really understand how the Treasury Department finances a deficit? If disbursements exceed revenues, obviously the difference must be financed. That is done on a continual basis when the Treasury anticipates a cash shortage and finances it through the sale of Treasury bills (short-term) and bonds (longer-term maturities). The mechanism for doing so is through a network of primary dealers—securities dealers that the Federal Reserve has approved to participate in the initial issuance of government securities as well as the execution of ongoing trading activities with the Fed.

The list of the primary dealers published and regularly updated by the Fed includes twenty-two banks as of this writing. These dealers are selected through a bidding process, and they are required to meet minimum liquidity and capital standards in order to remain on the list. They contract with the Treasury to market newly issued bonds to banks (themselves included, in the case of primary dealers who also have banking operations), corporations, pension funds, and individuals, establishing the initial market for the securities.

In addition, they maintain open communication with the Fed to provide information on current and anticipated market conditions in order to assist the Fed in developing monetary policy.

Primary dealers use an auction format to get Treasury securities (often called Treasuries for short) to market. Although Treasuries are only issued through these dealers, the mechanics are much like any other auction. Because the primary dealers are in tune with the market and their information is shared with the Fed, the issuance is a team effort of sorts, with the Fed directing rates and terms while the Treasury controls the volume being issued at a given time.

While the Treasury auctions are tightly controlled in terms of administration, the rates are still determined by the market. Let's assume the government is offering $10,000 ten-year bonds with a coupon rate of 6 percent. The market may be willing to bid only $9,500 for this particular issue. That would mean that the market believes that 6 percent is not a sufficient yield for this bond and values it (bids) lower, achieving a higher yield (6 percent/9.500 = 6.3 percent). Treasuries are initially issued through this primary-dealer network so that the entire market may decide the risk and reward ratio rather than the government itself.

If the market perceives that the government is spending too much and continually doing so by issuing more Treasury securities to finance that spending, the market will demand an ever-higher yield, thus paying a lower price, for new issues of securities. There are some differences in categories of bidders that allow more or less influence on the bidding process, but the important point is that, by offering the securities in an auction format, the ultimate control over rates lies with the market.

While the market does indeed control rates, the Fed certainly plays a role. The Fed, in times of low national confidence, may purchase Treasury securities in such great amounts that remaining issued Treasuries held by the private sector are insufficient to satisfy existing demand. This demand-versus-supply pushes prices for these securities artificially high, and their corresponding yield is artificially low. This can be true regardless of whether the Treasuries have existed for some time or are newly issued, financing current deficits. These Fed purchases enlarge the commercial banks' reserve pool, lowering the Fed funds rate to encourage borrowing and, hopefully, grow the economy.

Values of these securities still held by the private sector rise in response to reduced supply, and their corresponding reduced yield tends to push up the value of other financial assets held by the private sector. Of course, this isn't about economic fundamentals but government intervention. This can also cause critics to accuse the Fed of politicization, as citizens who own financial assets appear to benefit while others do not. If confidence is restored in society and the economy begins to grow vigorously, the dilemma is self-solving. If confidence is not inspired, the economy may stagnate indefinitely.

Though governments occasionally attempt to spur economic growth through deficit spending, this practice may culminate in the situation we have in the United States in 2014. We have the highest government debt-to-GDP ratio and the lowest GDP growth rate since WWII. While this is of concern, we should remember that government debt is mirrored by the private sector's savings, as bonds are just another way individuals, businesses, retirement-plan managers, and others store their savings. The private sector has chosen to loan its savings in order to receive interest payments. And while we can question whether holding large balances in Treasury securities is just an example of government borrowing crowding out investment in the private sector, the fact remains that there will always be demand for the safe-haven securities. Still, the historically high national debt is a reminder that monetary policy and fiscal policy must be in healthy equilibrium to inspire the confidence necessary to create continuous, well-balanced growth, as we do not want the government to overspend relative to GDP.

While equilibrium is certainly the goal, it is not simple to maintain. Just the word *deficit* causes concern. Many have an overall negative view of the government based on deficit spending alone. Indeed, many believe that the US economy is in worse shape than our politicians claim. If we believe the media headlines, we may be headed for catastrophe.

Despite what journalists may say, however, the United States will not go bankrupt, simply because it is impossible for it to do so unless it chooses that path. The Treasury is not like a business or even our individual households, where we have a limited amount of income and resources that must be balanced with our spending or we become insolvent. Because it has a unique position as the issuer of its currency, the Treasury can actually spend without regard to its income, financing its deficit spending by issuing debt or relying on the Fed to supply funds as needed. What does this mean? Simply that, if the government requires more funds, it authorizes the issuance of more Treasury securities.

What about the debt ceiling, you ask? Well, while it does limit the ability to issue more debt, it serves more of a political purpose than a practical one. The parties in Washington may blame one another, but at the end of the day, they will do what is necessary for business to continue as usual.

What happens when all of that Treasury debt becomes so large that the United States cannot meet maturity obligations, as the pundits warn? Won't the government go bankrupt then? Of course not. There is not likely to be a sudden shift in the market whereby the holders of Treasuries demand to cash out. Most Treasury securities are rolled into new ones at maturity, so they really just continue on. And while demand does fluctuate somewhat, Treasuries are going to remain attractive as savings vehicles because they are backed by the US government, making them quite safe.

If the market did suddenly move away from Treasury securities, the government would honor those obligations. Because the United States has a fiat currency system and the government directs the issuance of its own currency, it does theoretically have the ability to direct the Federal Reserve and the banking system to provide it with needed funds. It would certainly be inflationary to do so, and we know that our system currently does not operate that way, but the option to avoid bankruptcy is there.

Not only is there a mandate for primary dealers to always participate in auctions of Treasury securities, but, with Congressional authority, the Treasury can obtain direct funding from the Fed. While this would only occur in an emergency situation, it certainly is an available remedy if there was a time of crisis. So the government will not run out of money unless it chooses to do so. It cannot go bankrupt, because its spending is not constrained by solvency. However, it cannot disregard the effect of unrestrained spending on the overall economy, namely inflation, which would be the result of funneling too much liquidity into the economy at a given level of productivity. The Fed must always keep its eye on the overall level of national debt relative to GDP. While many political debates reference the mounting debt being handed down to future generations to repay, the real concern should be the ratio of debt to our national productivity.

Think for a moment about the concept of borrowing. Typically, we borrow in order to accelerate the ability to afford something we want or need. In business, we borrow in order to grow productivity more quickly than we otherwise could. If that productivity is healthy, then the business will prosper. In the case of government spending, if a country is leveraging wisely, using deficit spending as a way to grow GDP at a faster but still healthy rate, then the debt incurred is beneficial to overall living standards. As America's national debt has mounted throughout history, so has the country's standard of living.

There will always be differing opinions on the validity of government programs and deficit spending, and we will not optimize it all of the time. But America's historical success can be viewed as evidence that when deficit spending is funneled wisely into productive channels that permit the private sector to flourish, GDP will rise along with the country's average standard of living, benefitting current and future generations. If government spending is irresponsible, then we would expect to see living standards stagnate along with GDP. That is the burden we do not want to place upon the shoulders of our grandchildren.

So rather than focus on the amount of government debt

accumulating, which is the tagline used by politicians, we should pay attention to the efficiency of the government's spending. Wise spending, such as beneficial infrastructure or defense spending that maintains global peace and prosperity, will pay off for generations to come in terms of increased output, which will improve the ratio of debt to GDP. And that brings us back to equilibrium. Once again, we see that the key to maintaining a healthy economy is the balance of the three pillars that we discussed in the first chapter.

Clearly, the Federal Reserve and the US Treasury play key roles in the way our economy works. While technically independent of each other, they coexist in such a way that they work in harmony to accomplish the overall goal of maintaining stability in our economy. Without one, the other would be less effective; the sum is perhaps greater than the parts. But as important as their roles are, they do not, and cannot, act alone. As stated in the introduction to this chapter, our goal is to better understand the economy, and we cannot attain that without a clear working knowledge of how the banking system operates. Having now developed a familiarity with the roles played by the Fed and the Treasury, we have laid the groundwork to move into a discussion of the commercial banking system and its importance in our economy.

# CHAPTER 4

## MONEY, BANKING, AND THE REAL ECONOMY

We have probably all heard the phrase, adapted from a Bible verse but commonly repeated, "Money is the root of all evil." In reality, money is the root of the modern economy. Once upon a time, people carried out their business primarily within their local communities by trading goods and services with each other in a barter system rather than using any medium of exchange. Money allows us to trade beyond our local economic circle by valuing goods and services in terms of a common unit of exchange.

This expansion beyond our local community is further enabled by the commercial banking system, which allows us to carry out transactions all over the world. We can see evidence of the larger, global economy as we go about our daily lives. The Internet places the ability to make purchases and transact business all over the world literally at our fingertips. Just imagine what our forefathers would think if they could see the way computers have revolutionized the business of banking!

For most of us, cash transactions are becoming more and more infrequent. Some smaller retailers still trade primarily in cash, but most businesses function by way of checks, bank drafts, or wires. At the register, checks are being replaced by credit or debit cards that are linked to bank accounts, and the ease with which we swipe our cards is a testament to how dependent we are on the banking system. But beyond the mechanics of a checking account, most of us do not really understand how the commercial banking system works. Gaining a basic understanding of the way the banking system operates can enlighten us to the mystery of money creation and the way it functions within our economy.

## BANK REGULATION AND OVERSIGHT

With the economy operating on a global scale, oversight is needed to ensure that checks and balances are in place and stability is maintained. A financial crisis in a smaller country that has little international impact may be no more than a blip on the world's radar screen, but a banking-system failure in a larger economy such as that of the United States, China, or the Eurozone could result in a meltdown of epic proportions. To prevent major banking disasters, all central banks in the largest nations in the world are members of the Bank for International Settlements. Commonly known as the BIS and based in Basel, Switzerland, it is called a *central bank for central bankers*. Formed in 1930, the BIS is the world's oldest banking and financial organization, and its role as a stable advisor and resource in monetary and economic matters is well established.

The heads of Federal Reserves and central banks of various countries convene regularly in Basel to discuss global coordination of monetary behavior, with an end goal of fostering an environment that encourages each country to be at relative equilibrium with other countries, thereby helping ensure that there will be proper credit supplied and available to the global economy. Over the last several decades, the Basel conventions have produced various rules and regulations that have been mutually accepted and implemented by most countries. Known primarily as the Tier I, Tier II, and Tier III Capital Ratios, these actions seek to provide a basis for measuring and regulating bank capital. Simply put, they determine how much a commercial bank may lend relative to its capital base.

If a bank's portfolio of risk-weighted assets were to become too large and a significant portion of those loans defaulted, the loss from that default could wipe out the entire capital of the bank. This could literally put banks out of business and possibly threaten the banking solvency of a nation. By establishing ratios for measuring the amount of capital a bank must maintain on its balance sheet relative to the amount of loans it has outstanding, the BIS establishes a system of checks and balances that promotes global economic stability in an increasingly dynamic political and financial climate.

## BANK RESERVE REQUIREMENTS

As we know, banks act as depositories that hold funds in safekeeping for customers either in savings or checking accounts. These accounts provide the means for individuals and businesses to pay bills and make purchases. Most of these transactions occur by way of checks or electronic funds transfers—Internet banking—so cash does not physically change hands. It is simply a matter of making the proper accounting entries when funds are deducted from one account and transferred to another.

But suppose a customer needs to make a transaction in cash. He may walk into a bank and ask to withdraw funds from his account or simply drive up to an ATM and access his account from the computerized teller. If a bank maintained little or no cash on hand, there would be no funds available for the customer. So there is a reserve requirement that directs the commercial banking system to maintain a certain percentage of deposits in cash. Generally, banks are required to maintain reserves roughly equivalent to 10 percent of total deposits, held in a combination of vault cash on hand and amounts on deposit at a Federal Reserve bank.

While reserves were originally put in place to prevent a run on the banks, which would cause depositors to panic and withdraw their money and could collapse the banking system, the primary function of reserve requirements today, from a bank's perspective, is to ensure that there is ample cash available to support daily bank operations. Because they are in the business, banks know the level of reserves that they must maintain. To ensure proper operations, they must maintain these levels without regard to the requirements being mandated by the Federal Reserve.

## THE BUSINESS OF BANKING

Now that we have an idea of the environment in which banks operate, we can move on to discuss the role that banks play in the money supply chain. The modern commercial banking system serves two primary functions. First, banks act as depositories, accepting deposits from customers for safekeeping and providing cash back to customers on demand. This function dates back to a time when goldsmiths stored gold for customers. We no longer have a gold-based economy, but we still seek to deposit our money for safekeeping and, hopefully, to earn a bit of interest while it rests in our account at the bank. Further, by keeping our funds in a bank account, we are able to easily transact for goods and services by writing checks, swiping cards, or entering payment information into our computers. Banks act as the clearinghouses for all of these financial transactions, settling funds between accounts.

Secondly, and arguably most importantly, banks supply credit to customers, lending funds to those seeking to borrow and then profiting from the interest and fees associated with the loans. On the surface, this seems to be a matter of providing basic service to customers. However, if we look a bit deeper, we come to realize that, by providing credit, commercial banks play a vital part in the creation and circulation of the money supply. In short, by creating credit, banks create spending power. And they do this, quite literally, with nothing more than accounting entries. While fairly simple, the concept seems to elude so many who fail to understand the basics.

## TWO KINDS OF MONEY

To understand how commercial banks create money, one must consider that there are actually two types of money. There is *base money*, which includes both the physical currency that we are all familiar with and bank reserves. Base money makes up a relatively small percentage of the total money supply. If you picture it as a pie, the wedge that represents base money would be surprisingly narrow considering that the mental image that comes to most of our minds when we hear the term *money* is a green banknote with a president's picture on it. This has been referred to as *outside money*, a term that is particularly applicable because of the fact that it is created under government authority (in the case of physical currency) or by the Federal Reserve (in the case of bank reserves), outside of the operation of the private sector.

The remainder, which is made up of what is referred to as *bank money* or *inside money*, is created inside the private sector and exists in the form of credit that is issued when banks make loans. Think of it as electronic funds—money that arises when an accounting entry is made to record a new loan. By issuing credit, a bank has given a customer new purchasing power. It is not cash and it does not increase the customer's net worth (because he also has a new liability to the bank), but it does provide the customer with the ability to spend. In a nutshell, this is how banks create money.

## THE TRUTH ABOUT DEPOSITS AND LENDING: WHERE MONEY COMES FROM

If you pick up an economics textbook, you are likely to see discussions of "fractional reserve banking" intertwined with the theory of a "money multiplier." In fact, many well-educated journalists and economists promote the money multiplier as the way that banks create money. Unfortunately, it is a misguided concept. While it once was true and it is still a valid theory, it is just that: a theory, one that is promulgated in textbooks and classrooms. As with many other ideas and theories, it is not our current reality, and it is not representative of the way banks actually operate in the modern economy.

According to the money-multiplier notion, a loan may be created when a bank receives a deposit from a customer. If we suppose that deposit was $1,000 and that the bank, we'll call it Bank A, had a 10 percent reserve requirement, Bank A would hold back $100 and then have $900 in fresh funds available to lend to another customer. Then, when the borrower of the $900 takes the money that he just borrowed from Bank A and uses it to make a purchase, such as a new car, it ends up being deposited in the seller's bank, Bank B. Now Bank B has a $900 deposit from which it will retain its 10 percent reserve requirement, or $90, and lend the remaining $810. Theoretically, this process would continue on and on until a terminal point is reached. It all sounds logical and it would be perfectly reasonable if not for the fact that banks do not lend based on deposits.

It's true: banks do not lend money that is deposited by customers. Your cash that you deposit in the bank for safekeeping does not become the basis of a new loan made to another customer. A bank does not have to have "loanable funds" in order to make a new loan. Therefore, the notion that they must hold back a portion of such funds before lending the difference is simply false. In actuality, banks lend based purely on customer demand and qualified credit. Then they seek to ensure that they meet reserve requirements after the fact.

Let's look at the mechanics of how it works in the modern banking system. If a customer who applies for a loan meets the bank's credit-approval requirements, the bank will extend credit to him. This is recorded on the bank's balance sheet with a debit to a loan-receivable account and a credit to the customer's deposit account. This makes sense, because the receivable from the customer is an asset of the bank, and since the bank has now effectively given the customer the right to demand the cash created by the loan, the customer has a new deposit account that is a liability of the bank. The loan led to the creation of the new deposit, not the other way around.

For example: Customer John Doe applies for a loan of $30,000 to purchase a new car. Bank A approves the loan. The bank's summary balance sheet just prior to making the loan looks like this:

| Assets | Debits | Credits |
|---|---|---|
| Loans Receivable | $1,000,000 | |
| Cash/ Reserves | 200,000 | |
| Total Assets | $1,200,000 | |
| | | |
| Liabilities and Capital | | |
| Customer Deposits | | $1,050,000 |
| Capital | | 150,000 |
| Total Liabilities and Capital | | $1,200,000 |

When the loan is made, the transaction will be recorded with the following entry:

| | Debit | Credit |
|---|---|---|
| Loan Receivable: John Doe | $30,000 | |
| Deposit Account: John Doe | | $30,000 |

Notice that no cash has changed hands. The bank did not need to have the funds on hand to loan to the customer. This is the "bank money" referred to earlier. Now, the reserve requirement is still in effect, and the new deposit that was created when the loan was issued has now increased the bank's required reserves by 10 percent of the loan amount. If the bank does not have excess reserves already, it can seek to meet its requirement by luring new deposit customers from other banks—often by paying competitive rates of interest on the deposits (hence those large ads we see hanging outside banks' doors)—or by borrowing reserves from other banks who have excess reserves to lend.

Because reserve requirements are determined based on an average of a bank's deposits over a set period of time, banks are able to carry on their day-to-day operations by lending first and finding reserves later. In this example, reserves are adequate to meet the 10 percent requirement both before and after the loan is made. Let's take a look at the bank's summary balance sheet after the loan is made:

| Assets | Debits | Credits |
|---|---|---|
| Loans Receivable | $1,030,000 | |
| Cash/ Reserves | 200,000 | |
| Total Assets | $1,230,000 | |
| | | |
| Liabilities and Capital | | |
| Customer Deposits | | $1,080,000 |
| Capital | | 150,000 |
| Total Liabilities and Capital | | $1,230,000 |

You can see that the only balances that changed were the loans receivable and the customer deposits. Cash and reserves did not change hands at all. Now, of course, if John Doe actually spends the loan funds by withdrawing cash, those funds would leave the bank, and the total reserves on the bank's balance sheet would reflect that decrease in cash on hand. But that would happen regardless of the type of funds being withdrawn.

Similarly, if a customer writes a check from his checking account, funds are issued from the bank either in cash or by electronic entry. So cash and reserve balances change continuously all day long without regard to any loans being made. Keep in mind, however, that when loan funds leave one bank to purchase a car, they end up being deposited in another bank, increasing that bank's reserve balance. So, if we view the banking system in the aggregate, as if it was one big bank with lots of branches, the total loans, deposits, and reserves would be the same, with the funds just shifting among the branches. The funds will continue to circulate through the economy until the loan, whether in part or in full, is eventually paid back.

Since we know that adding to the money supply requires creation of a new asset, it follows that the money supply can only contract when an asset is destroyed. Since the borrower repays the lender with an existing deposit, an asset is being removed each time a payment is made. Therefore, the deposit that was created when the loan originated is extinguished when the loan is paid back, completing the cycle of money creation.

Think about how banks operate. You do not walk up to a teller's counter when you apply for a loan. Lending decisions are handled by a separate department. Every day, while loan decisions are being made, cash deposit and withdrawal transactions are continuously being processed. If a bank could only make a loan if reserves were held in adequate amounts, it would be like a tiger chasing its own tail. Considering the number of branches operating for most regional banks, there would be no consistent way to determine cash on hand in a real-time manner in order to either approve or deny a loan request. Loans are always made independent of reserve balances.

Of course, in practice, a bank's upper management would have a general idea of where reserve balances were hovering. And there are different levels of approval required for loans over certain thresholds. But these management practices are in place to keep things running smoothly and efficiently, not as a function of reserve requirements. As is required by federal regulations, the bank will ensure that it still meets the required reserve balances based on periodic historical measurements. There is a look back for a certain specified period, usually around two weeks, to determine the bank's average total deposits. An average of the cash and reserve balances for that period is calculated to determine if the bank is in compliance.

## ROLE OF THE CENTRAL BANK

So what happens if a bank falls short of its required reserves? Since we have established that banks do not lend their deposits and that loans are simply electronic funds created with accounting entries, it is clear that banks do not lend their reserves to customers. However, they do lend reserves to one another. If a bank has excess reserves on hand, as in the previous example, it can put that money to work earning interest by lending its excess reserves to a bank that needs reserves to meet its 10 percent requirement. This is not actually a loan in the context of extending new credit to increase purchasing power, as with a loan made to a bank customer. It is simply shifting reserves that are not needed to another bank who needs them and charging that bank for the right to use them. It is similar to charging rent for the use of an asset. In this case, one bank is essentially renting reserves from another.

Who controls all of this? Recall that reserves are made up of cash on hand (vault cash) and balances in reserve accounts at the central bank. It is the Fed that is charged with management of the overall reserve pool by way of the interbank market. If one bank has excess reserves and another needs to borrow to meet its reserve requirements, the net result is a shift from the reserve account at the Fed held by the former to the reserve account of the latter. Again, no physical dollars actually change hands. It simply comes down to journal entries.

Bear in mind that all of this is reflected on the central bank's balance sheet where the deposit accounts are maintained. While each bank has its own balance sheet that shows its reserve account as a debit balance (because it is an asset of that bank), the central bank reflects the opposite side of each entry. Deposit accounts are liabilities of the entity holding the funds. If you have funds deposited at your bank, the bank owes that money to you when you ask for it. So the reserves held on deposit at the Fed are liabilities of the central bank, because they are owed back to the individual banks who deposited them there.

Picture it this way: Assume the banking system is made up of three banks—A, B, and C—plus a central bank.

CENTRAL BANK
Deposits (Liabilities) $1,475,000

COMMERCIAL BANKS

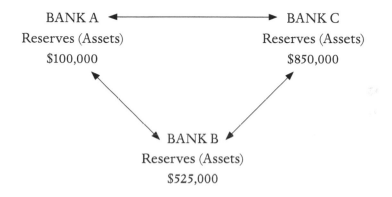

BANK A ←———————————→ BANK C
Reserves (Assets)               Reserves (Assets)
$100,000                    $850,000

BANK B
Reserves (Assets)
$525,000

The total deposits shown on the central bank's balance sheet is obviously the sum of the reserves held by each individual bank in the commercial banking system. Each bank maintains its reserves on the assets side of its balance sheet. Conversely, that account shows up as a liability on the central bank's balance sheet. So a look at the central bank's balance sheet reflects a liability for the aggregate amount of reserves in the commercial banking system.

Simply put, there is a pool of reserves spread around among the different banks. This pool is constantly circulating among banks. When one bank borrows from another bank, it simply shifts reserves from one to the other without disturbing the overall size of the pool. But that doesn't mean the size of the pool never changes.

Since we know that banks make loans based on credit and without regard to reserves, it's easy to imagine a scenario in which the pool of reserves in total would fall short of the required reserves needed by the banks in aggregate. When this happens, the central bank steps in and increases the size of the reserve pool.

To understand how the central bank controls the pool of reserve funds, it helps to understand the makeup of the central bank's balance sheet. Basically, the liabilities of the central bank are made up of the following:

1. Reserve accounts attributed to individual banks
2. The US Treasury's deposit account
3. Currency in circulation (because cash is a store of value that is backed by the government)

US Treasury securities make up virtually all of the asset side of the balance sheet. That is the key to the central bank's ability to adjust the size of the reserve pool.

How does it do this? Recall that one of the duties of the Federal Reserve is management of the nation's money supply. The primary mechanism in its toolkit is *open market operations*, which is the term given to the purchase and sale of Treasury securities by the central bank. Carried out by the Federal Open Market Committee (FOMC), open market operations can be used to either expand or contract the reserve pool in circulation. If more reserves are needed in the aggregate banking system, the FOMC simply authorizes purchases, through open market channels, of treasury securities held by a commercial bank. Purchases are recorded by accounting entries that reflect deposits of newly created central-bank money in the reserve accounts of the selling banks.

It is an asset swap of sorts, whereby the banks just exchange Treasury securities for newly created reserves. The bank's balance sheet changes in terms of asset makeup, but its net worth remains the same. Of course, the banks are selling interest-earning securities, but they receive new reserves in the process. If they have sufficient capital and market demand is healthy, they will replace their securities with higher-earning commercial loans. The end result of the open market operations is that the banking system has a larger pool of reserves, which will be shifted around as needed to meet aggregate reserve requirements.

Because the Fed can purchase securities by way of accounting entries debiting the central bank's balance sheet and crediting the commercial banks' reserve accounts, no money actually changes hands. The central bank just purchases the securities with newly created electronic "money." The Fed has the backing of the US government, so it has the unique ability to create money out of thin air with a simple journal entry.

Conversely, if the Fed determines that the commercial banks' reserve pool is too large, it will sell Treasury securities. All of this can be executed quickly, allowing the central bank to respond to changes in loan demand, as well as other factors that tell it when increases or decreases in the reserve pool are warranted. As we have established, reserves are a function of loans, not the other way around. The central bank supplies reserves as needed to allow the banking system to meet aggregate reserve requirements. That makes it very clear that reserve requirements do not constrain lending activity.

## LENDING IS CAPITAL CONSTRAINED

So what *does* act to control lending practices and keep banks from getting out of control? Ultimately, a bank's capital will curtail lending. Looking at a balance sheet, capital is the difference between total assets and liabilities. That is simple enough, but what does it mean? Think of a bank's capital as a type of cushion. If the bank was liquidated and all liabilities were satisfied, the capital is the amount of assets that would remain. Since it represents the amount of the bank's assets that would be there after liabilities were paid, it is the cushion available to protect it in case of a decline in the value of the bank's assets.

But how does the capital relate to lending? Remember the Tier I, Tier II, and Tier III ratios issued by the BIS? Basically a measure of a bank's capital relative to its outstanding loans, the capital ratio provides a risk-weighted measure that determines when a bank needs to slow down lending. Leverage ratios measure the bank's capital against its unweighted total assets.

Obviously, banks make money when they make loans to customers. Since they do not have to have deposits to lend and they can find reserves to meet prescribed requirements, banks could keep on loaning as long as there was demand for borrowing. With demand being a function of the market, a healthy economy and a competitive lending-rate environment could allow a bank to easily find itself with an abundance of customer demand. As long as the spread between interest rates on new loans sufficiently exceeds the rate that a bank would pay to borrow any reserves it might need, the bank stands to profit. Since banks' profits increase as their lending activities increase—because as profits grow, capital grows—it makes sense that they would lend every dollar possible.

However, if a bank has too much risk outstanding relative to its capital, it is jeopardizing its overall health and teetering toward possible insolvency. Moderate, balanced growth is the better alternative, allowing capital to grow along with profits, resulting in a gradual increase in loan portfolios. Typically, that is what happens. Whether it is accumulation of profits or acquisition of investors that increases a bank's capital base, it provides a foundation for expansion of the bank's loan portfolio. Reserve levels do not come into play because the bank knows it can find reserves as needed to back up deposits created by extension of qualifying loans.

From a practical standpoint, loan officers are authorized by upper management to make loans up to a certain amount, with that ceiling being determined based on the bank's capital, granting them room to do business without being required to request specific permission to make each individual loan. Assuming customer credit risk is being responsibly evaluated and managed, it is capital and leverage ratios, and not reserve requirements, that keep check on how rapidly a bank expands its loan portfolio.

## BENCHMARKS AND TARGETS

Now that we've discussed how and why money is added to the economy through the banking system, let's take a look at what happens when it gets there. As we know, the Fed strives to achieve target employment levels and maintain mild inflation, and it adjusts the money supply as necessary to accomplish these objectives.

Recognizing that the creation of money is an accounting concept—in that this money is created and moved around the system literally with accounting entries recorded in computers—it seems like a simple, matter-of-fact idea. In fact, the larger issue is not a question of "How do I get the money into the system?" but of "How much money does the system need?" How much is too much? How much is too little? Where is the healthy balance?

We have all heard that too much money creates inflation. The well-known saying "There are too many dollars chasing too few goods," which implies that inflation is a function of the money supply, is simple but relatively correct. The word *inflation* generally has a negative connotation, even inciting fear for some, especially if they lived through the 1970s. At the same time, we are led to believe that inflation is good. It can be confusing. So how are we to know when inflation becomes a bad thing?

The Federal Reserve has learned through observation of economic activity over time. We have had one hundred years now since the Fed's founding in 1913 to learn about how money affects an economy and how much money the economy needs. Just like Goldilocks, we want it to be not too hot, not too cold, but just right. Historically, it has turned out to be true that 2 to 3 percent inflation is a good thing but more than that is unhealthy. In order to achieve this sweet spot, the Fed takes the appropriate action, primarily through the FOMC, to drive the economy in the correct direction.

We often hear that the Fed sets interest rates, but that is actually not true. The Fed sets the Federal funds rate, which economists on the FOMC decide upon based on the environment in which the economy is operating at the current time. Commonly referred to as the "Fed funds rate," this is the interest rate that lending institutions charge to borrow reserves from each other. Further, it is the benchmark rate upon which other lending is based, directly impacting other short-term interest rates as well as the prime rate, which is used by banks to build rates for longer-term borrowing.

But how does the Fed implement its target rate? It simply uses open market operations to nudge the rate toward its target. The Fed looks at the volume of overnight lending between banks and from that is able to get a read on the overall demand for reserves. If the reserve pool is too small, the demand from banks pushes the interest rate up. If the pool is too large, rates shift downward in response to decreased demand for borrowing. Since the central bank has an interest in maintaining a reserve pool balance that allows it to achieve its target interest rate, the Fed supplies reserves as necessary to meet the demands of the commercial banking system, which in turn pushes the Fed funds rate toward its target. Since we know that the central bank does not seek to restrict the amount of bank reserves supplied into the system, rather injecting reserves as needed to meet the aggregate demand necessary for banks to maintain the reserve requirements indicated by new deposits being created, it is clear that the Fed can use the demand in the reserve "market" to control its benchmark rate.

In recent years, the Federal Reserve has implemented another measure to help control benchmark rates. Legislation passed by Congress in 2006 authorized the Fed to begin paying interest to commercial banks on excess reserve balances. This was not a new idea; in fact, it had been around for decades. Although the timing made it seem as if the "interest on reserves" notion was somehow related to the stimulus program rolled out in response to the recession, it actually was passed earlier with the intention of supplementing monetary policy by offering an additional way for the Federal Reserve to control the Fed funds rate.

By paying interest on reserves, the Fed is able to increase reserve balances without concern that it will push the Fed funds rate lower than targeted. Although the rate is minimal, by paying the banks some interest, the Fed is converting excess reserves into income-producing assets for the banks. That tends to slow interbank lending activity during circumstances when that is of concern, and it makes banks more amenable to maintaining excess reserve balances.

While the legislation was originally passed in 2006 and scheduled to be implemented in 2011, it was accelerated by the 2008 Emergency Economic Stabilization Act. This move proved to be particularly important for monetary policy, as the need to flood the banks with reserves in response to the banking crisis saw excess reserves at historic highs and pushed the Fed funds rate to historic lows. The interest rate on excess reserves effectively establishes a lower boundary on the Fed funds rate, helping the Fed fine-tune its target.

Because the Fed funds rate serves as the base rate upon which other lending rates are built, the Fed can use it as a trigger point to control the overall inflationary pressure in the economy and maintain a healthy equilibrium. When the Fed funds rate is low, interest rates on loans tend to decline, encouraging borrowing. This fuels the economy. If the Fed determines that stimulus is needed, it can inject reserves into the pool and drive the Fed funds rate down in an attempt to make consumers more interested in obtaining new credit.

The opposite effect happens if the Fed tightens reserve balances and allows the Fed funds rate to adjust upward. By influencing the overall demand for borrowing in the economy, the Fed can exert some control over the money supply, thus helping control inflationary pressure. The Federal Reserve Board understands that it is targeting a rate at which the system will achieve the ideal balance to encourage moderate inflation, but not so much that it will become overheated and allow inflation to grow unchecked.

## MORE ON INFLATION

Perhaps the most famous quote about inflation came from the late Milton Friedman, a much-respected economist at the University of Chicago who stated that "inflation is always and everywhere a monetary phenomenon."[3] Since inflation is understood to be a rise in the average prices of goods and services in the economy, that summation seems almost too basic. Of course inflation is a monetary phenomenon—it's about money! But just as different academics have argued over time about what really causes inflation, misunderstandings persist even in our modern economy.

Friedman theorized that inflation is all about the money supply. How much money is in the system? Too much money will create inflation; too little will create deflation. As a monetarist, he believed that a restrictive money supply, too inadequate to feed the natural behavior of the economy, would cause prices to fall because too little money chasing too many goods would result in a situation where supply exceeds demand. Conversely, if there is too much money in the economy, prices will increase in response to demand, which is outpacing supply. When presented this way, it seems quite logical. This is a prime example of a theory that can be best explained with a clear understanding of the way that the modern monetary system actually works.

So what really causes inflation? This is a key economic question. After all, if we understand what triggers a specific event, we can prescribe the best methods to prevent it from happening. Friedman was partially correct: inflation does in fact bear a relation to the size of the money supply in the economy. While monetarists will argue that there is a causative effect, most economists who base their theories on the mechanics of the modern monetary system believe that increases in the money supply are likely to be a reaction to inflationary pressures or, sometimes, a corollary occurrence with inflation but not actually the cause.

Think about the way the money supply is adjusted. While central bank intervention might increase the money in the reserve pool or alter the mix of assets in the economy through open market operations, the overall money supply only expands when new credit is created by the banking system. The demand for credit would only stem from a need to increase manufacturing output or perhaps a desire for investment or consumption. But the increase in demand would always be ahead of the extension of credit; therefore, it is demand for new loans that leads to increases in the money supply. Since we know that demand for credit is a function of confidence in the economy, we could actually say that confidence plays a much more critical role than the money supply when it comes to driving inflation.

As the catalyst for loan demand, confidence is key when consumers make purchasing decisions. If a buyer fears that prices will soon increase, he may feel inclined to accelerate a purchasing decision. While it is fear of inflation that motivates that purchase, there must be confidence to support the choice to go ahead and borrow the funds. Similarly, if a consumer believes prices are stable, a purchasing decision may be deferred. If he has concerns about his economic future, his confidence will falter, and he will not be motivated to take on new credit.

Does this mean Friedman and all of the other monetarists were wrong? No, it simply means that they may have misunderstood the interplay between credit creation and the money supply. As with some other schools of economic thought, they may not have grasped the way that the modern banking system works and its primary role in the creation of money. They may have missed the fact that, without demand for credit, the money supply simply cannot increase. Those misunderstandings may have fueled a belief that increases in the money supply could be forced. Still, there are lessons to be learned from those who have penned economic thoughts and theories through the years, not the least of which is that a basic familiarity with accounting and banking is essential to understanding the way the economic world works.

So if inflation is not a function of the money supply but more a reaction to economic confidence and demand, why are we led to believe that inflation is a bad thing? The mere mention of inflation in a headline causes immediate fear and concern, painting a picture of falling portfolios and rampant price increases. In truth, inflation is a bit like an out-of-town visitor, tolerable in small doses but wearing out its welcome if it hangs around too long. We do need a moderate amount of inflation, because without it the economy would suffer from stagnation. A thriving economy will naturally evolve with a touch of inflation—a sign of increased productivity—as it moves forward. A healthy rate of inflation is evidentiary of an economy that is accomplishing more with fewer resources, thereby increasing GDP.

History proves that the ideal economic equilibrium with optimum GDP expansion requires an inflation rate of around 2 percent. When inflation hovers in that range, the economy has enough forward momentum to drive productivity yet keep prices in check, ensuring sound growth. And steady growth feeds right back into the level of confidence in the economy. So while experts like Milton Friedman propose that inflation is a function of the money supply, a clear understanding of the banking system leads us to take it a step further. Yes, changes in the money supply may be related to inflation. But they do not cause it.

Prices are generally a function of supply and demand, and price inflation can happen regardless of changes in the amount of money in circulation. Increased demand for certain categories of assets, such as oil or building supplies, may push up prices throughout the economy. Changes in the availability of resources, such as fuel or agricultural produce, can affect the supply of goods, which will also result in price inflation. And, yes, increases in lending can drive prices up if the resulting increase in spending power is not balanced with growth in productive output. Healthy economic growth is a balance of credit expansion and increasing output and GDP. The key is balance, and the catalyst is confidence. If those elements are in place, there will be a natural rate of inflation that drives the productive engine of the economy.

## QUANTITATIVE EASING

We know that the central bank will feed reserves into the system as required to meet demand. How can it ensure that the banking system as a whole does not continue lending beyond a point that is healthy for the economy? Is there a point at which the Fed would simply stop supplying reserves? From a practical standpoint, the answer is no. The Fed is motivated to supply reserves as needed in order keep the Fed funds rate at target. After all, the Fed's end goal is to maintain healthy inflation and employment levels.

That leads us to consider quantitative easing, or QE as it is often called. With the recent recession still fresh in our minds and news reports, most of us are quite familiar with the term, which sounds very sophisticated and powerful. But beyond a basic understanding that it has something to do with trying to help a sluggish economy, most people do not really understand what it means. Very simply, it is open market operations on a grand scale. Before such measures are undertaken, the Fed would have, through normal open market operations, targeted the Fed funds rate as low as it could feasibly go. If that has not sufficiently bolstered consumer confidence to encourage spending, QE could be initiated in an attempt to give the economy a nudge.

In order to provide liquidity for the banking system, the Fed initiates the purchase of Treasury securities in exchange for reserves. The mechanics are basically the same as the routine open market operations carried on by the central bank, with the distinction that, in QE, the securities being purchased may include longer-term Treasuries as well as mortgage-backed securities, municipals, or other financial debt instruments, and the amount of bonds being purchased is predetermined with a specific time period for execution of the plan. Basically, QE is an asset swap in which the Fed provides liquid reserves to banks in exchange for less-liquid securities. Basically, the Fed is pumping up bank reserves.

Now we know that simply feeding reserves into the system will not increase credit or trigger increases in loans. Only customer demand for borrowing will do that. If banks are not loosening credit standards, borrowing will remain stagnant. And if the economy is wrought with fear and uncertainty, indicating a lack of consumer confidence, customer demand will not increase. From a consumer's standpoint, borrowing entails risk, and a prudent person will not undertake new risk without confidence that there is an upside. Confidence inspires the courage to take on risk with an eye toward future growth. New borrowing translates to an increase in the money supply. Without confidence, the banking system stagnates. It is that simple.

So given the massive amount of reserves pumped into the system with QE1, QE2, and QE3, what is the purpose of QE? Most news reports maintain that stimulus money is intended to rekindle GDP growth, energize the private sector to spend money, and push the economy forward. Some of the government bailout programs did serve to bolster the private sector. But the degree to which QE accomplishes those objectives is a point of debate, and economists often disagree on the overall effectiveness of the program. While it is possible that certain categories of assets, such as real estate or bonds, could see a bump up in value if the Fed purchases related securities in the open market, causing a slight increase in demand, the direct effect of QE is minimal. After all, the real end effect is that the balance of equities held by the banking system has been altered by virtue of swapping one asset (Treasury securities, mortgage-backed securities, etc.) for another (reserves), but the total of net equities held has not changed at all. Without an increase in loan creation, the money supply is not increased.

We can look to the recent rollout of QE as an example. While there were variables, such as the fact that some of the equities purchased with QE1 were severely discounted (i.e., mortgage securities) as compared with QE2 or QE3, it is evident that the expected stimulus in terms of credit expansion did not happen. What QE did do was help stabilize the banking system.

The economy was spiraling into recession, and unemployment was on the rise. As real estate began to lose market value, the rate of borrower defaults increased. Banks' loan portfolios quickly lost value, throwing capital ratios off substantially. Faced with a drop in income as well, many banks were clearly in trouble. By pumping reserves into the system, QE propped up the banks by providing liquid assets (reserves) while at the same time sweeping their balance sheets clean of some of the battered subprime mortgages purchased by the Fed as part of QE1. To the extent that it stopped the trend, this helped hold bank insolvency (i.e., assets valued too low to cover liabilities and cash levels inadequate to meet demands) at bay.

As banks regained stability, some of the public's confidence in the viability of the banking system was restored, but overall, the effect of QE on the economy was negligible. This is evident in the fact that QE1, although aimed at supporting the credit market, had little economic impact. Additional phases were subsequently rolled out as QE2 and QE3, both of which focused on purchasing Treasuries rather than mortgage-backed securities, and both of which simply added reserves into the banking system without much, if any, real economic impact, other than helping maintain low borrowing costs for the Treasury. Most of the reserves poured into the banking system have remained there as excess reserves, meaning that banks' lending portfolios did not increase.

Some argue that it was all for naught, although keeping the reserves in place served to maintain stability in the banking system through a slow period of recovery. As for the factors behind the outcome of QE and its overall success as a matter of policy, the debate will continue and economists will surely have differing opinions. The one certainty is that we can learn from watching history unfold so as not to repeat our mistakes in the future.

## MORE ABOUT INTEREST ON RESERVES

In good economic times, the interest paid on reserves is just part of the Fed's toolkit. In times of crisis, it provides the Fed with the ability to pour reserves into the system while still maintaining a floor on its target rate. During the recent recession, the Fed, with its QE programs, made monumental attempts at stimulus. Yet because of a pervasive lack of economic confidence, loan demand did not materialize. Banks were in a holding pattern. With few new profitable loans being issued and their Treasury securities now sitting at the Fed, their profit margins were being squeezed. Implementation of payment of interest on excess reserves, while intended to be an addition to the Fed's toolkit, served a secondary purpose of replacing some of the income banks had formerly received from their Treasury securities.

As the Fed tapers its Quantitative Easing program, talk of unwinding its bond purchases continues to draw attention. Some believe that it will lead to economic instability or inflation. Since we understand that loan creation and the money supply is not affected by the size of the banking system's reserve pool, we also understand that tapering QE will not lead to inflation. However, the markets may react to perceived changes in Fed policy, and that may lead to instability. Therefore, the Fed must use caution and employ various tools to control the Fed funds rate as it alters its program. The interest paid on excess reserves allows the Fed to control the rate more accurately and quickly. Effectively serving as the lower boundary, the interest rate paid on reserves makes it easier to fine-tune the rate, providing the ability to make adjustments without changing the levels of reserves.

## CROWDING OUT

Economists frequently use the label *crowding out* to describe what happens when an increase in government spending results in a corresponding decrease in spending and investment in the private sector. Whether it is due to expansionary fiscal policy or a reduction in tax revenues, deficit spending leads to government borrowing. Some economists hold that this borrowing pushes interest rates up, resulting in a decrease in demand for borrowing in the private sector, therefore a reduction in private investment that affects unemployment and the supply of goods and services. Other economists propose that crowding out is more often seen as a function of competition when an expanding government encroaches on the private sector by using up goods and services that would otherwise be available for private-sector consumption. For example, when a growing government creates new jobs, the labor pool available to the private sector is decreased as workers shift toward government employment. Or if investors see government bonds as safer investments and purchase more Treasury securities than securities issued by the private sector, more funds are directed to government spending than for private-sector investment and innovation.

Economists differ as to the importance of crowding out and the extent to which it actually occurs. Some feel that government absorption of resources can only impact the private sector to the extent that the growth in government deficit spending outpaces the growth in output of resources. Others consider any shifting of a class of resources from the private sector to the government to be part of the crowding-out effect, as in the case where increased government borrowing pushes interest rates up and drives demand for private-sector borrowing down. The supply of financial resources may not change and overall demand remains constant, but resources shift toward the government.

Regardless of economists' differences in definition or opinion, it is clear that crowding out is largely a function of the overall economic environment. Consider that, in a time of recession, sudden increases in government spending might be prescribed as necessary to kick-start a sluggish economy. Would that spending increase result in crowding out? If interest rates are already low and economic demand is lagging behind supply, it probably would not.

In the most recent recession, deficit spending increased substantially, yet the stimulus actions did not drive up interest rates or crowd out private investment. With excess capacity already in the economy, few if any resources were shifted away from the private sector. Instead, the increased government demand for resources simply soaked up available supply in the economy without driving up overall demand. Since there was no competition for resources between the public and private sectors, crowding out did not occur. Conversely, when the economy is operating at capacity and growing, any increase in deficit spending that leads to government borrowing could result in competition with the private sector for goods, services, or investors.

## VELOCITY AND OTHER ECONOMIC INDICATORS

Economists define the money supply in terms of layers that build successively upon each other, moving from the most liquid to the least. The narrowest layer, called *M0* or the *monetary base*, includes actual cash in circulation and reserve accounts at the central bank, while the broad categories of M3 and M4 encompass larger, longer-term deposits, including institutional funds. M2, the term most often used when talking about money, includes all notes and coins in circulation, cash equivalents, and cash accounts except for time deposits of $100,000 or more, so it is fairly representative of the currency available to us to carry out our daily activities. But why does keeping a measure of the money supply matter? Many economists believe that the size of our money supply can be used as a guide to understanding and predicting both short-term economic variables and longer-term movements like inflation, helping Fed officials determine the appropriate course of action in terms of monetary policy.

To view the money supply as an economic indicator, one must recognize that it should be expressed in terms of its relationship to other economic measures. For example, we find that historically, M2 multiplied by approximately 1.6 equals the *gross domestic product* (GDP), with GDP being defined as the total output of goods and services for, typically, a one-year period. So if M2 = $10 trillion, GDP would be approximately $16 trillion. That means each dollar is spent approximately 1.6 times in a given year—a *monetary velocity* of 1.6. Since 1.6 is the typical velocity, if M2 or GDP change so that velocity drops to 1.4, it would mean that money is turning more slowly and producing less relative GDP. This could signal an outbreak of inflation, because there is now surplus M2 in the economy relative to the norm. As the commonly repeated theory goes, if there is too much money chasing too few goods, the result could be price inflation or even an asset bubble.

Since a decrease in velocity just means that money is circulating relatively more slowly, it could also mean that there is a lot of money parked in bank accounts and not being used for consumption or investment, possibly because of a lack of confidence in the future or possibly a fear that the economy is overregulated. It comes down to common sense: If there is a fixed supply of money and an economy is thriving, there are lots of economic transactions and money is changing hands more frequently. If economic activity has cooled, or if there is an increase in the supply of money, each dollar changes hands less often.

So it makes sense that velocity can serve as a gauge of the overall health of the economy, because it generally is evidentiary of the rate at which the economy is growing. While it can provide useful insight, it should always be examined along with other economic measures, such as the size of the money supply, to provide the necessary context to make sense of the situation at hand. Where the size of the money supply can drive prices, velocity should be seen as a signal or a symptom of other economic conditions, but it does not bear a direct causal relationship to factors like price inflation or asset bubbles.

This is not meant to be a statement about the proper amount of money supply or rate of velocity, because the definition of *proper* would be a moving target based on the economic, political, and social fundamentals in place at a given time. This should be viewed as simply an attempt to provide understanding of some effects of changes in the money supply and how the velocity of that money can impact the overall health of the economy.

Another measure of economic interest is *capacity utilization*. From an economic standpoint, capacity utilization is the extent to which production capacity is being employed. It is an indicator of efficiency, in that it represents the amount of output actually being produced relative to the total output possible at a given cost of production. Economists keep an eye on the capacity utilization rate, as it is often believed to be a predictor of inflation. It has been observed historically that approximately 82 percent capacity utilization will result in a low unemployment rate and relatively stable prices. Historical graphs and charts illustrate that at around 85 percent, that relationship no longer holds true, making an outbreak of inflation more likely if other economic variables are in place.

Notice the use of the word *historical* in relation to the 85 percent benchmark. While the capacity utilization rate has long been a key economic indicator of interest to economists, its applicability has been questioned in recent years. In fact, data from the 1990s to the present seems to indicate that the relationship between the capacity utilization rate and inflation is much less stable than previously thought. Economists once believed that capacity-utilization rates over the 85 percent mark signaled a greater likelihood of manufacturing bottlenecks and competition for resources, which would lead to supply-chain problems and place upward pressure on prices, hence the common use of the measure as a warning sign of inflation. Now, that predictive power is less clear.

Perhaps that is due to the somewhat obvious fact that any measure of production capacity would be heavily weighted toward manufacturing industries, a segment that is shrinking in importance to the American economy. With the world becoming more globalized, much manufacturing has shifted overseas, and information and service industries have become more prominent in the United States. Information services need less capacity, therefore technology and innovation can enhance GDP without a corresponding increase in capacity. While the importance of the capacity utilization rate in terms of predicting inflation in our modern economy may be unclear, the takeaway is that this measure of production capacity is one of many economic benchmarks available to those attempting to gain a better understanding of the way the economy works.

No discussion of basic economic indicators would be complete without inclusion of the unemployment rate. This should ring especially true with all of us who paid attention to the most recent recession in America. Even after reports announced that we were in recovery, forecasters were cautiously focused on the unemployment rate, which remained stubbornly high. Each time the government released a jobs report, eyes turned to Wall Street and the anticipated market reaction.

From an overall perspective, the rate of unemployment, defined as the percentage of the labor force that is actively seeking work, tends to be a lagging indicator of economic health. If the economy begins to dip toward recession, businesses tighten their belts and unemployment rises. As more businesses contract or fail, more jobs disappear. The result of the job losses is like a domino effect, impacting both the public and private sectors of the economy. Individual incomes drop and fewer income- and payroll-tax dollars are paid into the system. Lower incomes mean less spending, which affects local businesses as well as local governments, which rely on sales-tax revenues to meet budgetary demands. When jobs are lost, fear and uncertainty infiltrate all areas of the economy, pushing confidence aside and painting a bleak picture of the future. As we know, confidence is an essential element without which an economy cannot thrive. Regardless of what other factors might be in place, if jobs are scarce, confidence will not prevail.

Clearly, the unemployment rate is a significant indicator of the current mind-set in the job market. It is a mathematical measure of unrest in that it defines the percentage of the workforce that cannot find employment. But it does not tell the whole story. What about the people who are not seeking work? Shouldn't a study of productivity in an economy consider individuals who are able to work but, for whatever reason, choose not to pursue employment? The *labor-force participation rate* is another employment statistic that the Bureau of Labor Standards monitors and publishes. Basically, it is the measure of the percentage of the labor force that is currently working or actively seeking work.

The labor force is typically defined as those between ages sixteen and sixty-four who are physically and mentally able to work. By looking at the percentage of this pool that is either working or seeking work, thereby participating in the labor force, we can gain a different perspective on the overall health of an economy. There will always be individuals who choose not to seek employment, whether they are in school, raising children, finding satisfaction in volunteer endeavors, or simply do not wish to work. As the average age in a population changes, there will be gradual changes in the makeup of the labor force.

Changes in the labor-force participation rate serve as signals to economists. If the rate decreases, it could mean there are sectors of the economy that have permanently contracted. Or perhaps more individuals have simply given up and are no longer trying to find work. By viewing the unemployment rate in tandem with the labor-force participation rate, we can gain a better understanding of the condition of the employment sector and get a reading on the labor market, which, when combined with confidence, truly is the heartbeat of any economy.

## ASSET BUBBLES

We've discussed how price inflation can break out in the overall economy when the demand for goods exceeds supply. However, perhaps a more dangerous problem is that of asset inflation that is not the result of an excess of overall demand but rather of excess dollars being funneled into a certain category of assets. Why? When prices for a particular asset, such as housing or gold, are continuously bid upward based on expectations of future growth, borrowers are able to borrow more and more on that artificially inflated collateral. Whether due to a flight to the perceived safety of a certain asset category, such as bonds, or investment opportunity, such as rental real estate, sudden spikes in demand can result in quickly inflating prices. The artificially created values are unsustainable in the long term, and prices are bound to correct. At a certain point, borrowers cannot support the higher loan payments and the falling collateral values are insufficient to meet bank loan to value ratios, causing banks to call many of those loans.

This is exactly what happened in the 2008 housing crisis. Riskier lending products, such as subprime mortgages and the use of mortgage-backed securities to fund much of the expansion of housing-related debt, compounded the problem. But at the core of the crisis was a buildup in housing values that was fueled by loose lending standards and low interest rates, allowing more and more borrowers to qualify for loans. The American dream of home ownership became accessible for more people, but the quality of much of the new lending made for an unstable foundation. It wasn't a problem while the housing market was booming and things seemed great. But then the music stopped all at once, or so it seemed.

What led to the fallout? When a few houses in a neighborhood are in distress or foreclosure at any given time, it will not affect the values of all the other homes. However, when too many houses are distressed at any one time, a tipping point is reached. Market values are determined largely by comparable sale prices. Too many foreclosures or short sales will drop the average, resulting in lower market values for all of the remaining houses in the neighborhood. This may upset the required loan-to-collateral ratio of lending institutions that hold mortgages on the affected homes. Suddenly, loans are *under water*, meaning that the amounts owed on the properties exceed the values of the underlying collateral. Under pressure by regulators, lenders begin calling those loans, accelerating payment of the entire balance, even if the payments are current, possibly pushing more homes into foreclosure. As banks' income streams taper and balance-sheet ratios become unhealthy, the systems freeze up and a widespread deflating spiral in value begins.

Real estate is just one asset category that can become overpriced. Think about stocks and bonds. When money is available at favorable rates and easily attainable credit standards, it can help to bring about speculation in investment markets. Think about it. When money is tight, people buckle down and stay the course. They may hold more cash and liquid assets. If money is available, they begin seeking alternatives. If borrowing is easy and you are not worried about income, you will tend to put money in the place that offers the potential for the largest return. That means you look to the asset category that seems to indicate rising values, often taking on more risk as you do so. If many participants in the market move into a particular category at the same time, demand may outweigh supply and prices will climb, creating a bubble.

Your investment advisor knows all about bubbles and may encourage you to invest in both stocks and bonds for diversification, and to weigh each according to expectations of growth in value of one category and avoidance of loss in the other. This can be sound advice, especially if it entails spreading risk while also capitalizing on more rewarding sectors of the market. That being said, an investor should consider the economy as a whole before making any significant investment decisions. If a relative surplus of M2 is in the economy at a given time, bubbles may form, and diversification may not prevent massive losses.

For example, when there is more money circulating than currently needed to fund productive output, people will begin to look for opportunities. If that money begins pouring into investment markets, both stocks and bonds may become overpriced simultaneously. If bubbles form and burst, market diversification will not prevent widespread fallout. And bubbles may form quite quickly. Potential investors may have money parked in CDs or other lower-yielding financial products. The owners of those assets, seeking a higher yield, may shift their money out of low-yield products and purchase assets like stocks and bonds. Once this shifting starts, stock and bond prices will be continually pushed upward as demand for the assets exceeds supply. As values inflate, the assets' fixed yields will reflect an ever smaller percentage yield. Clearly this cannot continue indefinitely, as an overpriced market will correct.

This scenario could occur in most any market. Whether real estate, technology, or even very specialized goods like yachts, any market can develop bubbles if sudden demand drives values up. The stock market is particularly vulnerable, however, because it is fairly easy to enter and the average investor may have difficulty monitoring factors like supply and demand. So what should one do to avoid being caught up in a bubble? Other than relying on advisors, stock-market investors look to various economic ratios and statistical measures when evaluating stocks or bonds.

One such indicator is the price/earnings (P/E) ratio. Historically, the US stock market has sold at a P/E ratio of around 15. That means that if earnings per share of a particular stock are, say, $5, that stock may sell for a price of $75 (75/5). A P/E ratio of 15 produces a 6.7 percent return (5/75). If that same share of stock is pushed up in the market to $100, the P/E ratio rises to a dangerously high 20 (100/5), and the yield is pushed down to 5 percent (5/100). While this may happen in one stock without significant impact, inflated P/E ratios for an entire market segment could signal a maturing market or indicate the sudden formation of a bubble that may threaten an investor's entire portfolio.

A good story about an overpriced stock market based on an excess of available money comes from just before the great stock-market crash of 1929. Joseph P. Kennedy, patriarch of the Kennedy clan, was having his shoes shined one morning on Wall Street. His shine boy began giving him stock tips. Kennedy listened thoughtfully. Upon finishing his shoe shine, he left the stand, called his stockbroker, and said something along the lines of, "Sell all my stocks and hold the proceeds in cash!" Soon enough, the market crashed, and many investors lost everything.[4, 5]

Kennedy's reasoning was simple, and it applies to this very day. If even an unsophisticated investor was buying stocks, all other would-be investors were most likely already invested in the market. Any economic event of good news couldn't push stocks higher, since there were no more buyers, yet any market-upsetting news could cause investors to begin selling, and doing so in an ever downward spiral, dropping values severely. When the market did indeed crash, Kennedy, who was flush with cash, began buying distressed securities and other assets on his way to becoming one of the wealthiest men in America.

Another example, which illustrates the impact of far too much lending into an economy, relative to GDP, happened in Japan in the 1980s, pushing asset values to absolutely staggering heights. I remember being astounded by, and have never forgotten, an article that began with this heading: "Tokyo Worth More Than All of California." You know how that was destined to end, and it did.

A recent reminder of this type of liquidity-fueled spending binge sits in my garage. A vintage V-12 Ferrari, in every way identical to mine, would currently be listed for sale at over seven times the amount I paid for mine twelve years ago. That is an annually compounded rate of almost 18 percent! Can that make any economic sense whatsoever—a forty-plus-year-old Italian car that leaves oil droplets on my immaculate garage floor appreciates at nearly 18 percent while the US GDP growth rate for the same period is about 3.8 percent? Does that reflect my investment savvy? I only wish that I could claim that. The obvious truth is that cheap, easy, abundant money has pushed these values far too high.

When passive investments begin producing returns that we might expect to see from an actively managed and successful hedge fund, it is a sign that there is far more money in the economy than is needed to service current output levels. Instead of fueling production, some of that money found its way into the vintage-car market. Hey, but it is a beautiful old classic Ferrari. New problem: my wife says it's time to sell!

## LOOKING FORWARD

With so many opinions and conflicting reports circulating about the economy, it's no wonder that so many people find it confusing. Traditional relationships of the money supply to some of the often-used economic indicators have become skewed in recent years, leading some to question their applicability as tools. Indeed, many who are well versed and educated in economics are often confused. In trying to make sense of it all, the experts will track the multitude of economic indicators and attempt to predict what the economy is going to do next. But things change quickly, and it is difficult to hit a moving target.

Sometimes measures undertaken do not play out as expected—as with recent efforts at stimulus, where the intended outcome may seem logical from a textbook standpoint but other factors come into play. We are often left with as many questions as answers. At the end of the day, it all really comes down to confidence. Many economists and others believe that when citizens, including employers, fear that fiscal policy and monetary policy are not conducted in a sensible equilibrium and are not perceived to be pro-growth for the economy, those citizens simply lose confidence in the future.

The resulting fallout can be widespread, from decreases in spending to rising unemployment. Until confidence is regained, spending will remain sluggish. Rather than hire and invest in productive activities, which would entail much risk in times of uncertainty, business owners may tighten up their spending for fear of an uncertain future. When they are seeking safer alternatives for their money than growing their businesses, they tend to invest (speculate) in financial assets (stock, bonds) and collectibles (like old Ferraris). Of course, as there may be more and more buyers interested in certain asset classes, the value of those assets is pushed higher and higher, giving rise to the belief that the wealthy are getting wealthier, even though it's really just rampant speculation driving the values upward.

These buildups in value can be very fragile, and the difficulty is to predict when they are going to peak and move out of some markets. Corrections can happen gradually but are more likely to happen with a short period of steep decline. A little hiccup may occur, causing buyers to panic and prices to plummet drastically. The speculative buildup in value is truly fragile and could burst at a moment's notice. That is why we use the very fitting term *asset bubble*.

# CHAPTER 5

## GLOBAL MONETARY LINKAGE

I'll begin this chapter with a primer on currency trading. Suppose a US citizen wants to purchase something from a seller in Germany and have it shipped to his home in the United States. Whether the buyer purchases the item directly from the seller or buys it through a US importer, let's assume that the seller will expect to be paid in euros, the currency of the Eurozone, of which Germany is a member. In order to complete the purchase, the buyer (or the importer) would need to exchange US dollars for the equivalent amount of euros.

To do so, he could utilize the services of a bank, which would have access to the currency market through *forex*, short for *foreign exchange market*, a worldwide decentralized market for the trading of currencies. Through forex, the buyer could simply exchange into euros the number of dollars needed for the transaction—for a small transaction fee, of course. This is a typical transaction that happens around the world billions of times per day.

# EXCHANGE RATES

The mechanics of currency exchange are really quite simple. In our example, the American buyer of German goods exchanges dollars for euros in order to transact business with the German seller. Now, in our digital age, we can purchase goods from overseas just by logging on to a computer or even a smartphone, so we may not actually have to go through the process of physical currency exchange. Still, whether we actually go to a bank or use digital bank transactions to buy goods, the process is essentially the same. We are using our domestic currency—dollars—to purchase an equivalent amount of foreign currency. It is a swap based on the prevailing market exchange rates at the time we execute the transaction. Quite simple, yet very confusing for those who do not understand how the foreign exchange market works.

# THE SPOT MARKET

The larger and more important point is not how the exchange is made, but rather, who or what controls the exchange rates of these many different currencies. The market does, of course. But how does the market know which currencies, on any given day, are worth a little more or a little less than they were yesterday, relative to another currency? It comes down to supply and demand, which is a function of current economic factors, political activity, and general confidence in one currency's potential for future performance relative to another. Uncertainty or instability may upset economic confidence, resulting in suppressed demand and falling values. The currency market is typical of others where the many influencing factors converge to result in an exchange known as a *spot deal*.

To understand how the spot market works in terms of determining value for a particular currency, let's consider a simple scenario using the US dollar. To set the stage for our example, let's back up a bit and look at the economic big picture of the United States. Let's say that for 2014, the annual GDP (from the US Department of Commerce) is projected to be around $15 trillion. With a few keystrokes, we can quickly access Internet data that tells us that the average money supply (M2) is $10 trillion. Remember that M2 is simply cash in circulation plus the amount of money that has been loaned into the economy by the commercial banking system and is now spread out into millions of bank accounts owned by you, me, businesses, and so on. Those accounts are on the banks' books as deposit liabilities (a credit on the bank's balance sheets because the bank owes them to the account holder upon demand). So, we have:

$$\frac{\$10\ trillion\ M2}{\$15\ trillion\ GDP} = 66.6\%,\ or\ 67\%$$

We awake the next morning, go to the web over coffee, and see explosive good news! The headlines of two newspapers with worldwide circulation, the *Wall Street Journal* and the *New York Times*, exclaim, "Cancer Cured! American Company to Make New Drugs Available Immediately!" and "New Oil Extraction Techniques Discovered by Texas Innovators: Gas Prices to Drop to 75 Cents per Gallon in Three Months!" Wow! Obviously, these examples are absurd, and they are meant to be. But the immediate reaction of all the world economists, currency traders, and everybody else who reads and cares is to expect an unbelievably great 2015. They may envision something like this: a 2015 GDP of $20 trillion!

With the $10 trillion outstanding money supply (M2) to be circulated within a $20 trillion GDP, the ratio changes to:

$$\frac{\$10 \; trillion \; M2}{\$20 \; trillion \; GDP} = 50\%$$

The result, it would initially seem, is that each dollar circulating in this economy can buy more goods and services. Obviously, and immediately, each dollar becomes worth more, assuming that all else remains unchanged. But the reality is that each dollar becomes worth more very quickly as foreign investors buy dollars with which to invest in US assets like stocks and real estate, expecting to profitably benefit from this rapid growth. Of course, domestically, intense loan demand by consumers and investors would increase our M2 over time, restoring the M2-to-GDP ratio.

So, is this great for the United States? Yes! Besides the obvious positive impact of such news, it makes each of our dollars able to buy more euros or other currencies. If we want to purchase something from Germany, it will cost fewer dollars to buy that item.

Other factors could affect the dollar in a different way. For example, if the GDP appeared to be continuing on the same path as before, lacking that 2015 expected explosive growth and assuming that everything else remained the same, the trading value (exchange rate) of the dollar could remain the same. Or it could strengthen for a different reason than rapid growth, such as a policy change.

For example, if the Fed decided, in its infinite wisdom, that too much money was in the economy, it could tighten its monetary policy, removing excess reserves through open market operations, selling from its portfolio of Treasuries (assets on the Fed's balance sheet) to various commercial banks. This would be nothing more than an asset swap; it would not change the overall values on bank balance sheets, but it would remove liquidity from the banking system's reserve pool, putting upward pressure on interest rates, thereby discouraging some lending. The slowdown in lending, combined with the reduction in deposits resulting as loans were paid off, would decrease the amount of money circulating through the commercial banking system, thereby reducing overall M2 in the economy. Of course, with fewer dollars in circulation, the value of each dollar would begin to rise.

So while some factors may be unexpected or unplanned, policy makers do sometimes have a hand in the amount of money in the economy. And although Fed actions may not be specifically aimed at controlling the value of the dollar, the impact is sometimes a byproduct of monetary policy changes.

With just a few examples, it is easy to see how many factors come into play each day that affect currency values. Of course, overall economic outlook plays a major role, as does political stability, both at home and abroad. Really, it all comes down to confidence in the future. Good and bad news throughout the world, the behavior of various countries' central banks, as well as lending behavior by the commercial banks all send signals to the currency markets on a continuous basis. With real-time reporting and reactions to such events, constant world currency revaluation should come as no surprise.

## PURCHASING POWER PARITY

Economists and currency traders, as well as participants in international markets, keep abreast of certain market indicators in order to predict movement in foreign exchange rates. One such indicator is the measure of *purchasing power parity*. Really a theory, it suggests that exchange rates between currencies tend to push toward equilibrium. A basket of goods valued in one currency should cost the same in another, after adjustment for currency exchange.

What does this mean? For simplicity, imagine that a pizza pan costs $100 in the United States. What would that same pizza pan cost in Mexico? If the prevailing exchange rate indicates that one dollar is equivalent to 12 pesos, you would expect the pan to cost 1,200 pesos, right? What if you find out that Mexican companies are selling identical pizza pans for 800 pesos? If you own a chain of pizza parlors, wouldn't you be motivated to purchase the pans from Mexico? Assuming the products are equivalent and shipping costs are not an issue, then of course you would take advantage of the savings opportunity. And if that is the case, purchasing power between the dollar and peso is not at parity.

While this may seem like a great opportunity for someone who is in the market for pizza pans, we must consider the long-term effects of disequilibrium. Demand for pizza pans sold by US companies would drop as those sales shift to Mexican companies, and therefore the demand for pesos would increase. This would place upward pressure on the value of the peso relative to other currencies. The increase in demand would push prices for Mexican pizza pans up. At the same time, to compete with Mexican companies, US companies would have to begin reducing prices for pizza pans in an attempt to attract customers. As the prices for pizza pans moved up in Mexico and down in the United States, they would eventually reach equilibrium.

The values of the currencies would react to the changes and adjust as well, ultimately moving toward a natural state of parity. And while the overall market will not adjust because of the movement in prices for pizza pans, this same phenomenon is taking place across all markets all the time. Furthermore, if the purchaser is not one retailer or a regional restaurant chain but a giant like Walmart, then the stakes are suddenly much higher and the impact is greater. Cost savings become much more meaningful at that level, and business decisions will be motivated by those savings opportunities. It is yet another example of how human nature comes into play in our economic lives.

Markets shift and businesses respond, capitalizing on savings where they can while looking for the next opportunity. The common truth is that, absent intervention, markets eventually move toward equilibrium, proving the theory of purchasing-power parity. This is the point that those market watchers understand. They watch for changes in certain market segments and then use that information to make predictions about upcoming trends in the currency markets.

## TRADING FOR PROFIT

As in our example, the currency-trading market evolved in accommodation of a necessary step in the process of transacting business with another country. It was nothing more than a means to an end. These days, when we read or hear about the foreign exchange market, we are most likely talking about something completely different. As with most other business and profit-making ventures, currency trading originated from a combination of opportunity and innovation. Foreign exchange trading, made possible by modern banking and communication systems, has become one of the fastest growing investment market segments.

The basics of currency trading are fairly straightforward. It is a business model that, like other trading and derivatives markets, has elements that resemble gambling. A trader is playing upon the constant fluctuation of currencies relative to one another, speculating that a particular currency will rise or fall in value. While it seems as if that should be a fairly simple bet, the underlying complexities of currency valuation make it a venture fraught with risk.

The industry is open to anyone, experienced investment managers and individual investors alike. With low regulation and no central market in control, the world of currency trading is fairly easy to enter. However, whether because they're intimidated or lack understanding of the way foreign exchange works, many smaller investors are hesitant to enter the currency-trading arena. Most profit-seeking trades are made by larger banks, investment managers, or hedge funds—the market participants with the most experience and access to the most reliable information. While the market exists to serve a specific business purpose, there is much speculative money to be made for those who truly understand the game.

While most individual investors will not ever participate in currency trading for profit, it is helpful to have some general knowledge about the way it works and the impact it can have on general economic conditions. There is no magic recipe. Basically, currency trades are executed in pairs, where the investor is simultaneously buying one currency and selling another. It is an asset swap, using one currency to purchase another. The opportunity for profit comes in when the trader speculates correctly and uses a currency that may be falling in value to purchase one whose value is rising.

Obviously, when the currency received in the swap appreciates, the trader profits. If a trader does this consistently, he can build up quite a nice number in his gain column. For larger and more experienced traders, leverage comes into play, raising the profit potential on the winning trades but also ramping up the risk for losses. And losses do indeed happen, with less than half of forex trades being reported as profitable.

So who are the players? The largest segment of the market, in terms of trading volume, is made up of banks. While banks of all sizes participate in the market in order to meet the needs of customers who are transacting business in other currencies, some also enter into the market for profit. Those with investment departments may be executing trades on behalf of clients, with a spread on the trade that represents the bank's profit. It is logical that larger banks, which hold substantial amounts of foreign currency anyway, would enter into the market in pursuit of gain. By using these currencies, that would otherwise be non-income-producing assets, to play the currency trading game, they can use the bank's own assets to bring in profits.

Since we know that exchange rates are a function of values as determined based on supply and demand, the size of the trades being carried out by larger banks often has a significant effect on the values in the currency-exchange market. With no central market in place, trades are essentially just bids and offers made between traders. A large bank can sway the price of a currency just by making a successful bid that will alter the value of that currency. While it may sway values only slightly, this still adds an additional element of risk to the guessing game.

Large traders place their bets based not only on their knowledge of expected government actions, anticipated central bank moves, political activities, expected economic performance of various countries, and the like but also by predicting what their fellow traders will likely be doing. While profit-seeking trades by institutional participants garner the most attention, a substantial amount of the activity in the exchange market is initiated by central banks and governments. Open market operations, typically aimed at affecting interest rates, often involve foreign-exchange activity—a central bank may purchase or sell foreign currency out of or into its commercial banking system to alter the size of the pool of currencies relative to each other, and thus their values. Government policies can drive the market in unpredictable directions, adding risk to the game for those who are in the market hoping to beat the average returns.

While most of us will not become currency day-traders, we should be aware of the impact that those who do participate in the exchange market have on currency values. Even the value of our dollar can be affected by these trades. While supply and demand for currency is the primary driver of value, the underlying factors that determine that supply and demand must be considered. Governmental actions and the like are certainly critical. But we must be mindful that movement in the currency investment market pushes values as well.

## EXPORTING INFLATION

Think back to the earlier example of dollars being traded for euros in order for a US citizen to purchase a German product. Does everybody win? The American buyer gets a better bargain, and the German seller gets a sale. End of story? Of course not. Generally speaking, leaders of countries—politicians—are always looking to improve their respective economies. If a country's domestic economy is performing satisfactorily but there is excess capacity available, whereby actual output is falling somewhere below potential, why not find a way to increase exports and expand the economy and GDP further? As long as it doesn't push too far and create an inflationary environment, it's a no-brainer.

All else being equal, here's how it works: Suppose a country, we'll call it ABC, endeavors to expand its exports and chooses to use monetary policy as a stimulus. ABC's central bank feeds reserves into the banking system through open market operations, essentially purchasing Treasury securities from commercial banks in exchange for new reserves that it creates out of thin air. The newly pumped-up reserve balance will sit in the bank's account at the Fed, so those funds will not actually filter out into the economy. However, the inflated reserve pool will drive the Fed funds rate down, which in turn serves to increase lending activity and create new deposits, which begin circulating in the private sector. That new money creation will result in more money serving ABC's economy, decreasing the value of each unit of its currency, as there are now more units out there chasing goods.

Over time, of course, the GDP will ramp up as a result of new productive investment. But in the short term, the relatively sudden increase in money in circulation will have a direct impact on the value of ABC's currency. This impact will spread to other countries by way of the foreign exchange market. Now that other currencies are relatively more valuable, those countries' citizens will be more likely to purchase goods from ABC. That may go on for a short time, but as those countries eventually begin losing exports to ABC, their central banks may take similar action and attempt to influence currency values to their advantage.

It is common sense, really. As other countries' purchasing power of ABC's exports increases and they begin to realize a decrease in their exports, they have two choices. Either they allow their local currency to continue to rise relative to ABC's and, thereby, continue to suffer losses of exports, or their central bank can take action to counter the currency's rise by stimulating an increase in their money supply. While initially addressing the exchange differential, the increase in the money supply will also create inflationary pressure. This is the meaning of the term *exporting inflation*. The actions taken by ABC's central bank resulted in a ping-pong effect, whereby another country, through its own reactionary measures, ended up with inflation in its domestic economy. The process will go back and forth as long as the countries are competing with each other, creating an overall tendency for worldwide inflation to creep up relative to worldwide GDP. Once the cycle begins, it is difficult to break.

So now, looking back at the example of the dollar vs. euro valuation, let's suppose that the US central bank executes stimulus measures intended to make the dollar more competitive. A German buyer would thus be encouraged to buy more US goods and, bingo, US exports begin to rise, uplifting our GDP. Good stuff for the United States! But what about German producers of goods and services? They expect to now lose some of their business, because the US goods are more competitively priced. In order to avoid a falling GDP, the German central bankers, as part of the Eurozone, will find a way to increase their own M2, erasing this advantage.

While it is possible that this type of activity could take place between two countries, it is far more likely that many countries would be carrying out these money games against each other. As the money supply of these countries gradually increases relative to GDP, the inflationary pressure will be felt by the worldwide banking system. While exporting inflation might not seem significant on a global scale when it happens to one country, the fact that it is a phenomenon that can affect all of the largest economies in the world at the same time makes it an international concern.

## THE EUROZONE AND ITS PROBLEMS

Having used the United States and Germany in the above examples, let's talk about the Eurozone, itself a trading bloc. Formed on January 1, 1999, the Eurozone is comprised of eighteen European area-member countries:

| | |
|---|---|
| 1. Belgium | 10. Portugal |
| 2. Germany | 11. Finland |
| 3. Ireland | 12. Greece |
| 4. Spain | 13. Slovenia |
| 5. France | 14. Cyprus |
| 6. Italy | 15. Malta |
| 7. Luxembourg | 16. Slovakia |
| 8. the Netherlands | 17. Estonia |
| 9. Austria | 18. Latvia |

The purpose was to create a trading bloc of countries unified by a common new currency, the euro, to increase trade with each other and with the entire world.

In economics, it is widely known that the use of one currency can significantly increase trade. The widespread benefits are logical: avoiding the transaction costs of exchanging currencies in the market, through forex, as well as the knowledge that one currency used within that trading bloc will not deviate in value from the time a transaction is contracted until it is completed. However, while originally conceived as a cure for fragmented Europe's economic ills, it has not been universally respected in idea or practice. Many economists believe there is a fundamental flaw. While monetary policy is coordinated through one central bank—the European Central Bank (ECB), based in Frankfurt, Germany—a unified fiscal policy (including government spending and regulation) was never fully implemented.

Primarily controlled by the governing bodies of each of the eighteen countries, the Eurozone has no strong and unified agreement regarding governmental fiscal behavior among its members. This problem becomes painfully apparent when some countries economically outperform others and some governments spend more, tax more, and borrow more than others. Think of Greece, and a few others, to be reminded of the economic chaos engulfing the Eurozone in this era.

If economists are beginning to understand the need for common fiscal governance, can we expect to see eventual economic success for the Eurozone nations? While anything is possible, it will take more than willing participants to solve the flaws in their union. In addition to the lack of fiscal unity, which is huge, the countries are faced with currency and budgetary constraints that stem from the fact that the individual members of the monetary union are not issuers of the currency that they use. In that way, they are much like American states. Yet we are different in that our states are all members of one monetary union with one national fiscal policy and a single Treasury that oversees monetary actions and is responsible for the production of the currency that we use. And that is key.

As an issuer of its own currency, the United States has the ability to manage budgetary shortfalls through Treasury security issuances, with the assurance that it will not default. While it may be inflationary, a currency issuer can always produce the money needed to settle its debts. Because the Eurozone nations have no ability to issue currency, they are faced with the real possibility of defaulting on debt, forcing borrowing from other member nations and others, and possibly straining relations.

Further limitations on the Eurozone nations' monetary autonomy come into play, ironically, because of the same fixed-rate exchange system that was designed to benefit trade. A floating exchange-rate system allows a country to implement policies to increase or reduce its money supply and, thereby, affect economic conditions like interest rates and inflation. Because of the way that a fixed exchange-rate system works, monetary policy changes lose a degree of effectiveness and trade rebalancing between nations doesn't occur effectively, even though the ECB advises each member nation on appropriate open market operations. The widely varying rates of productivity among the Eurozone members, even when disciplined by the marketplace, makes a unified currency a difficult objective to maintain. Without unified fiscal policies or a common treasury, the Eurozone countries are prevented from working toward a common goal. Despite being part of the same union, in many ways they are as much competitors as they are teammates.

With that bit of background, it becomes easier to see why the use of a single currency for purposes of trade has not provided the benefit the Eurozone countries were seeking. Each country is implementing the fiscal measures that it deems prudent to attempt to regulate its own economy. Because it is tethered to the other countries in its monetary union, it is affected by the policies being carried out by its fellow trading partners. Alliances between countries inevitably form, sometimes for mutual benefit in dealing with certain matters and other times simply to survive, and the lack of a common goal with unified focus makes it difficult for the union to thrive.

Although the member nations are in some ways like our states, they do not have the connection of shared history and pride in a national identity. Even if our states sometimes disagree, when it comes to matters of national importance, we unite like no other. The same cannot be said of the Eurozone members. Even if they were to eventually implement fiscal unity in name, they might never have unity in spirit. And that may be the biggest hurdle they must overcome if they are to achieve true economic success.

## GLOBAL ECONOMY

Everyone is aware of the way our modern world is connected. The Internet allows us to communicate globally in real time, making it possible to do business in ways previous generations would have never dreamed possible. This connectivity also presents us with challenges in terms of the way national economies are impacted by one another. The foreign exchange market is a prime example of the way technology has opened the doors for the development of a new business model. The effect that the market has on world currency values is not to be underestimated. Even if we do not participate in the market, we should understand how it works in order to makes sense of our economic universe.

Just as we all play a part in our local economy, each country is part of the global economy. Whether by governmental action or by business practices, the world's nations affect one another. When one country exports inflation, or when some governments over-borrow, it tends to create worldwide tolerance for greater and greater government debt, leading to the likelihood of that debt becoming more burdensome on a less-rapidly-expanding world GDP.

As anyone who has gone through a recession can testify, if a country—or the whole world—becomes over-leveraged, problems loom. It is a question not only of debt but also of living standards. Can we grow GDP faster to rebalance the economy? Can we reduce government spending as the cure? Should we employ a combination of both? We must look at the big picture.

The world is changing faster than some can keep up with. Technology and innovation are the driving forces behind much economic advancement. As the economies of emerging countries begin to grow faster, led by innovation, the global economy must adapt. Rapid changes in allocation and utilization of world resources can already be seen, affecting the supply-and-demand equilibrium. As economic standards rise for more people, the expectation of a higher standard of living will develop. Businesses will adapt quickly and address the demands that will stem from these expectations.

Governments must proceed cautiously, as global interconnectivity means that even seemingly tiny policy changes have greater capacity to impact not only a country's citizens but also the citizens of the world. Currency values are at the heart of almost every economic issue, both domestic and foreign. Even the slightest shifts in value can have worldwide impact. And in this age of instant communication, the effects of news can translate into changes in currency markets almost immediately.

More than ever, we must be aware of how interconnected our world has become. If we are to be part of the global economy, we must think and act globally. We must consider the impact that our choices will have on not only ourselves but on the world. And that begins with true economic understanding. In the next chapter, we'll look at an example of how one country's actions have affected the world's economy.

# CHAPTER 6

## THE GREAT CHINA STERILIZATION PROBLEM

No, I'm not talking about babies or a one-child policy. And I'm not talking about hygiene or cleanliness. I'm talking about economic subterfuge. This chapter is about monetary sterilization, a practice that is largely unknown to most people. Yet it is an everyday banking practice in China. It hurts the rest of the developed world badly and will eventually damage China itself.

There is disagreement as to the real impact of monetary intervention, largely due to a lack of fundamental understanding, and it should be pointed out that China is not alone in carrying on forms of this practice. Currency intervention has been used throughout history by many countries, including the United States, and countries like Korea, Japan, Switzerland, and others reportedly use forms of it today in an attempt to manage the value of their currency in the foreign exchange market.

So why do we care so much about China's practice and its impact on the world? It's partly due to the size of China's economy but primarily because of the difference in the way the Chinese carry out their methods. While other countries may undertake currency intervention, China carries it a step further, creating an unfair advantage over its trading partners. When one of the largest economies in the world unlevels the playing field, the impact is far-reaching. Given the ever-growing number of Chinese exports that we seek, the practice is particularly punitive to the United States.

## FURNITURE MELTDOWN

Before we dig into the practice of monetary sterilization, I'd like to digress into a bit of historical perspective.

I grew up in the Western Piedmont region of North Carolina, where I primarily live and work today. My CPA firm is based there, and consequently our client base through the years has included many of the manufacturing companies and other businesses that make up this diverse region. Some years ago, the number of furniture manufacturing clients began to seriously contract. Their sales fell, profits followed in a downward spiral, and more quickly than I could have ever imagined, these plants, one after the other, began going out of business. These companies had prospered for years, some for generations, and within less than two decades, they were gone, leaving behind a multitude of desolate, empty factory buildings.

These very companies had made this part of North Carolina into one of the primary regions for furniture manufacturing in the United States. It has some of the finest stands of hardwood trees in the country. The area has plentiful water coming off the mountains, creating rivers and lakes. This water helped nature produce very fertile soil, and high grade cotton came from this soil. The water allowed cotton mills to spring up here, there, and everywhere to enjoy the production of an early hydroelectric power boom. With plentiful hardwood forests, cotton, and hydroelectric power, an industry was born. Wooden case goods and upholstered furniture manufacturers were among the early job creators and wealth producers of this region. And now, after more than a century of productive prosperity, they were practically all gone!

## COMPARATIVE ADVANTAGE AND FOREIGN COMPETITION

A CPA firm is a window into the world of business. Clients in all types of businesses, large and small, enable us to see what works as well as what doesn't. Much of my time has been spent consulting with clients, hearing their problems, and finding good solutions to help them prosper into the future. But this hollowing out of the furniture industry so quickly was something I didn't fully understand.

Well, I did understand part of it: the economic law of *comparative advantage*. In a nutshell, this law states that if a producer of goods or services has a lower marginal cost than a competitor, he may have an overall cost advantage. *Marginal cost* is the change in total cost of production that arises when the quantity produced changes by one unit. The producer of other goods or services may have similar efficiencies in that which he produces. Those two producers each grow by trading with each other and enjoying the benefits of the other's specialization.

I easily understood that the furniture industry in the Western Piedmont area of North Carolina enjoyed comparative advantage with its abundant wood, power, and cotton. I could also grasp why China, with abundant and ultracheap labor, could enjoy that same kind of comparative advantage over the United States. As China industrialized and brought in very low- paid workers from their farms and trained them for factory work, the nation quickly became an industrial giant. But the magnitude of its comparative advantage was simply breathtaking. Even with early quality problems and transocean shipping costs, China was still killing us, economically speaking.

## CURRENCY STERILIZATION

In reaction to these rapidly occurring changes, I expanded my knowledge of how money works on a global scale and began to understand the power of sterilization. Very simply, the term *currency sterilization* refers to the practice of intervening in the foreign exchange market with the intention of maintaining the value of one currency relative to another, while also attempting to curb growth in the monetary base. Typically, intervention takes place when a central bank purchases foreign currency from its commercial bank system and pays for it by issuing new reserves, resulting in an increase in the domestic monetary base. If that central bank wishes to reverse that injection of new base money, it must employ tactics to adjust out the newly issued reserves, thereby sterilizing the change created by the intervention.

So sterilization is the second part of a two-step process. In China's case, it essentially involves efforts to control the exchange rate between the yuan and the US dollar in order to maintain the competitive advantage that the country currently enjoys, combined with efforts by the Chinese central bank to control the supply of base money. It is a complex process clouded by the fact that China does not readily release data to the world. This lack of transparency leads to speculation based on circumstantial evidence, as is apparent in the widely divergent information that can be gleaned from reputable publications. Combined with the often promulgated misunderstandings of the way the modern banking system operates, the lack of reliable information serves to produce reports that leave us with more questions than answers. But while we do not clearly understand all of the finer nuances of the practices carried out by the Chinese central bank, we have enough information, supported by corroborating evidence, to develop an idea of how China is sterilizing its currency.

Most politicians and journalists—and unfortunately many economists—miss the distinction between intervention and sterilization, and therefore they do not understand that the second step is the problem. It is a technical process that, quite frankly, can only be made clear with a working knowledge of modern banking and the fundamentals of a double-entry system of accounting. While we can examine the technical aspects of the way currency sterilization is carried out, we should attempt to understand the motives behind the actions, as that is the real concern.

Sterilization policy emanates from the monetarist theory that expansion in the money supply creates inflation. And when a country is experiencing large inflows of foreign capital into its domestic economy from export sales, excessive inflation is a valid concern. By controlling domestic inflation, China is able to suppress the natural rise in price levels that would result from its long-running trade surplus. But it comes at a price. The exploding growth in its exports, combined with its intervention in the foreign exchange markets, has resulted in quite a conundrum for China.

To illustrate how it appears that China is manipulating its currency and to distinguish between intervention and sterilization, suppose a Chinese manufacturer sells $1 million worth of goods to an American company. The Chinese economy is closed in terms of currency acceptance, requiring anyone doing business with Chinese companies to exchange their native currency for yuan. So the American company goes to the foreign exchange market, typically by way of a Chinese commercial bank, and exchanges its $1 million for the equivalent in yuan.

Two things have happened:

1. Money has been transferred from the United States to China in exchange for goods. Since the dollars were exchanged for yuan, which were already outstanding in the Chinese economy, the net increase in wealth is in the form of US dollars, which are sitting on the Chinese commercial bank's balance sheet as reserves from foreign exchange.

2. The supply (think of it as inventory) of dollars vs. yuan in the foreign exchange market has now shifted, resulting in a natural change in the relative value of the two currencies.

The introduction of more dollars into the foreign exchange market decreases the value of the dollar, thereby making the yuan relatively more valuable than before.

A weaker dollar would alter American demand for Chinese goods as well as make American goods more affordable for foreign purchasers. The blow to Chinese exports is made more severe by the boost to American manufacturers, a double impact that China cannot sustain if it wishes to maintain its competitive advantage in the world marketplace. Enter currency intervention. In order to maintain the targeted exchange rate and secure the Chinese balance of trade relative to US manufacturers, the People's Bank of China (PBOC), which is similar to our Federal Reserve, will purchase the $1 million that went into the foreign exchange market, and it will do so with newly issued yuan. The PBOC is essentially executing a swap with the commercial bank by taking the $1 million held in foreign reserves and giving the bank new yuan reserves in exchange.

The commercial bank's balance sheet position is restored with no change in net worth, and the PBOC's balance sheet has now expanded. The PBOC is essentially keeping the value of the yuan *pegged*, or linked, to the value of the US dollar. The PBOC could leave the intervention there and know it preserved the exchange rate at the desired target. However, Chinese officials fear that prices will rise in the domestic economy as a result of the newly issued base money, believing it will spur new lending. (Actually, the increase in deposits is really just a response to the new wealth that came into the country by way of the export sale.) *Sterilization* is the prescribed course of action to remove the newly issued liquidity (base money), and the PBOC executes this step typically with a form of open market operations whereby it swaps domestic bonds, often referred to as sterilization bonds, for the newly issued yuan reserves.

Let's review those steps in the context of sterilization. The classic definition of monetary sterilization is currency intervention that attempts to prevent the actions of a central bank from resulting in an increase in the monetary base. When the PBOC purchased the dollars by issuing new yuan reserves, the monetary base was increased by that amount. So to counter, or sterilize, the increase in base money, the PBOC must somehow remove the extra yuan that it created. This is most often done either through open market operations, similar to the way our Fed alters the reserve pool, or by raising the reserve requirements placed on commercial banks. With open market operations, the central bank sells domestic bonds to the commercial banks, thereby removing the base money from the pool. If reserve requirements are raised, it would theoretically increase the amounts, calculated as a percentage of their deposits, that the commercial banks are required to hold at the central bank, essentially suppressing the circulation of the reserves between banks.

Both of these methods are attempts to remove base money from the reserve pool and negate the effects of foreign exchange intervention, with an added intention of limiting the amount of reserves circulating in the banking system to support lending activities. If you are attempting to curb price inflation, as triggered by growth in your broad money supply, you would first look to reduce the rate at which banks are making new loans.

If you recall the discussion of the credit creation process and where money comes from in chapter 4, much of the previous illustration probably sounds contradictory to the notion that lending is not constrained by reserves. It is contradictory because it appears that the Chinese, like many classically educated economists in the United States and around the world, do not understand the actual mechanics of the modern banking system. Although we do not have particular statements to this effect, it seems clear in the obvious adherence to the idea that the money supply expands when banks lend based on a money multiplier. While PBOC officials do not explicitly state that they are attempting to stem lending of reserves, their actions imply that they believe that lending is reserve constrained. While we cannot discuss the methods that the PBOC uses in its sterilization practices without implying this theory, one should keep in mind the differences between its approach and what we know to be true in the US banking system.

While classical economic teachings promote such ideas as the money multiplier or the loanable funds model, both of which we know to be based on the premise that lending is dependent on existing deposits, not all such theories are entirely erroneous. Some just do not apply to the way the modern banking system actually works. For example, increases in the money supply can be inflationary, but the root of those increases does not lie in a money multiplier because banks do not lend deposits and lending is not reserve-constrained. But that does not diminish the concern for inflation. Rather than discard the entire idea, those who truly understand the modern monetary system suggest modification in approach, making the macroeconomic theories more relevant by boiling them down to mechanics in order to effectively apply them to the system within which we currently operate. By gaining a practical understanding of the way our economy works, we can separate the wheat from the chaff, filtering out the applicable truths and discarding the rest.

With that said, we can return to our illustration. Regardless of method, we know that China's primary goal is to maintain its competitive manufacturing advantage by artificially fixing the relative exchange rate of the yuan to the dollar and preventing price inflation in its domestic economy. It is clear that, whether by open market operations or raising reserve requirements, the PBOC is attempting to sterilize out the increases in its monetary base that occur as it issues new yuan reserves to buy up the US dollars pouring into the foreign exchange markets. Essentially, the foreign exchange balance is constantly upset, as China continues its pattern of net exports, requiring the PBOC to intervene in an attempt to restore the balance.

These transactions appear to take place on literally a daily basis, as the PBOC aims to maintain its control of the relative exchange value of the yuan to the dollar. It doesn't take a big imagination to entertain the volume of sterilizing actions required to counter these continued injections of yuan. In fact, we know that the PBOC has routinely carried out open market operations at a minimum of twice each week, often to the tune of hundreds of billions of yuan, to adjust the liquidity in the banking system's reserves.

While recent recessionary times have led the PBOC to inject reserves into the banking system, open market operations have typically been used to drain the liquid foreign exchange reserves that result from intervention. The ensuing buildup in domestic bonds on Chinese commercial-bank balance sheets translates into mounting interest costs that the PBOC must find a way to pay. Now, the PBOC is certainly not without resources. But what about all the US dollars purchased by the PBOC through its intervention practices? Resting in the PBOC's foreign exchange reserve coffers, the dollars are a non-income-producing asset.

In an attempt to offset the interest cost of the ever-increasing volume of outstanding domestic sterilization bonds, the PBOC often converts the foreign reserve dollars into income-producing assets by using them to purchase US Treasury securities, a relatively safe asset backed by the US government and one that is denominated in dollars, so the purchases do not affect the balance of foreign exchange. When you hear or read that the United States is in debt to China, this is what the journalists are referring to. While there are theories of sinister motives or underlying plans to control the US economy, the buildup of Treasury holdings by the Chinese can be directly tied to the PBOC's currency intervention and sterilization operations.

## WHAT ABOUT THE MONEY SUPPLY?

With all of this focus on reserves, it may seem that the PBOC has lost sight of the overall money supply. After all, the monetary base, as we know, simply circulates within the banking system as reserves. Money creation happens when banks expand their balance sheets with newly created deposits resulting from new lending. But what about the new deposits that are likely occurring as a result of the sales being made by Chinese exporters? Aren't those deposits creating money?

They do increase China's M2, which we know is defined as the total of bank deposits, short-term savings accounts, time deposits, travelers' checks, and the like. But M2 changes constantly as deposits move in and out of banks as part of normal business operations. While each deposit into a bank increases M2 at that point, the money being deposited was already in existence and was withdrawn from some bank at some other point in time, whereby it decreased M2. If the deposit moves from a foreign bank into a Chinese bank, it is just shifting from one place to another. Since there is no new extension of credit associated with the deposit, the overall global money supply does not increase.

However, this increase in M2 does add to money in circulation in China; thus, it can be inflationary in the Chinese economy. It should, in theory, be inflationary if it is in response to increases in productivity and GDP, just as economic growth is in the United States. As money moves into the country when it sells its exports abroad, productivity and GDP rise. As long as this rise is a natural evolution of healthy, moderate growth, it should be a seen as a positive occurrence. In fact, the healthy growth that results from productivity is what keeps an economy moving forward, although the Chinese government seems intent on suppressing any increase in the standard of living for its people.

Regardless of the perception of inflation and growth, the basic truth is that in order for an economy to expand, the money supply must grow through the banking system by extension of new credit. While the PBOC might be relying on classical economic theories and thereby undertaking the classic approaches to controlling growth in the money supply, it is accurate in its apparent focus on slowing the rate of lending by commercial banks.

If you understand the fundamentals of the modern banking system, you must be wondering why the PBOC seems to concentrate on using open market operations and high reserve requirements as its primary tools to manage the monetary base in an effort to control lending. This seems to imply, again, that the PBOC's approach is based on a belief in the mythical money multiplier. In the modern banking system, lending is not reserve-constrained. Capital requirements are the limiting factor for banks making new loans. If the banking system wished to slow lending, an increase in capital requirements would be almost instantly effective.

Another logical step would be to address credit-qualification standards. And in fact, the PBOC has at times implemented more stringent loan-qualification policies, sometimes requiring as much as 40 to 50 percent in down payments for new borrowing (this is particularly effective in stemming new housing loans) and enforcing credit quotas that result in rationing the extension of new lending. While we know that addressing reserve requirements and monetary base changes in the United States would not have much effect on lending beyond an impact on the Fed funds rate, we can really only make educated guesses about the Chinese banking environment. Maybe the PBOC is using many tools, and these are only the most apparent. Perhaps the PBOC is simply attempting to control the interbank lending rate (their version of a Fed funds rate) to suppress lending activities and using any means available to do so, although the required reserve ratio would have little to no impact in a system that is flush with reserves.

Perhaps banking regulations there cause the overall approach to reserve management to be different. For example, while we have no indication that this is the case, if the PBOC did not supply reserves as needed, banks would have difficulty in meeting stated requirements as they expanded their loan portfolios. Increases in the reserve requirements would accelerate the severity of that impact. Initially, the interbank lending rate would skyrocket, and ultimately a credit crisis could ensue. Of course, there would be other fallout, and the entire system would be in turmoil, giving us reason to assume that the PBOC has not enacted such a policy.

The fact remains that reports are often conflicting and underlying motivations are not apparent. Absent solid data, we must make assumptions about the restrictions and policies that the PBOC has implemented in order to makes sense of the motives behind its selection of monetary tools in a banking system that is far from transparent.

It should be noted that, under increasing pressure from world economic forces, China has eased reserve requirements placed on some smaller banks. It is stated that the motivation is to generate new lending activities. While we know that to be a misunderstood relationship, it likely would have little impact even if it was relevant, as the changes in requirements have been very small and only apply to a fraction of the country's banks.

## IT'S ABOUT SUPPRESSION

If moderate, sound growth is a sign of a healthy economy, why would Chinese officials be motivated to restrict growth by curbing lending? Wouldn't the government want to see its citizens' standard of living improve? Why is it so focused on suppressing growth? Clearly, the country has enjoyed the competitive advantage achieved through keeping the value of the yuan artificially low. This advantage has resulted in dramatic growth in China's exports since the 1980s. It follows that the domestic economy would experience an increase in the money supply along with an expansion of such magnitude. Growth in the money supply, after all, is a natural result of an expanding GDP, and a net exporter will experience growth as foreign currency comes into the economy in exchange for goods. As we know, if the money supply grows faster than GDP, which could happen if central bank actions were combined with economic expansion, excessive inflation can quickly follow, resulting in pressure on the yuan's value that could threaten the competitive advantage the country desperately wants to continue to enjoy.

Citing a fear of high inflation, the PBOC has placed its focus on keeping the value of the yuan artificially low while simultaneously fighting the battle of the increasing money supply. This must be a monumental task. By hindering the economic advancement that would be natural and expected in a country that is experiencing rapid growth in GDP, as has been the case with China, the PBOC is swimming against the current. While the Chinese government points to a fear of rampant inflation, the restrictive and detrimental nature of the PBOC's chosen methods ventures beyond management and into manipulation.

## RECESSION

While much of the PBOC's monetary policy activity remains shrouded in secrecy, more is being shared with the world, and there are some things that we do understand to be true. As we have already covered, the PBOC seems to focus on credit creation in an attempt to control growth, and it employs monetary policy to suppress inflation. We know that the PBOC has some of the same monetary tools at its disposal that the United States central bank does, such as open market operations and making adjustments in the reserve requirement ratio, although the latter is not commonly used in the United States. While the system is complicated by foreign-exchange intervention and sterilization activities, we know that the PBOC targets interest rates in a similar way to that of our central bank when it sets the Fed funds rate.

Though much of our discussion has focused on efforts to limit growth, it should be noted that China has not necessarily consistently restricted credit creation. Recession, it seems, can become a bit of a game-changer for a central bank that is otherwise bent on suppression. In fact, China's 2008–2009 stimulus package, which was rolled out primarily in response to the US recession, brought about a strong push toward rapid credit creation. The years between 2009 and 2011 saw increased pressure on Chinese officials to stabilize the economy. The reaction was to ramp up infrastructure and technological development projects in an effort to keep the economic engine churning ahead while at the same time tightening credit standards to curb lending in an attempt to prevent development of asset bubbles.

The years 2012 and 2013 were fraught with continued economic stresses for China, and the open market operations that continued twice per week often saw injections of liquidity into the banking system instead draining reserves by swapping bonds. This pushed lending rates down as reserve requirement ratios were reduced and credit standards were loosened—all in an effort to stimulate loan activity. Most of the new lending was directed toward the real-estate sector in order to bolster prices and prevent deflation in the market, which many believed to be overbuilt.

Now, as we know, a reduction in interest rates and a desire by banks to lend does not automatically create demand. Without confidence, borrowers will not take on new debt. Hence, the reason the US Fed's quantitative easing did little to spur new lending. With similar conditions in the Chinese banking system, especially after a long period of restricted credit, it would seem that easing policies during the stimulus would have brought borrowers in droves. When that didn't happen, the PBOC reportedly issued directives to the banks to lend, basically forcing them find ways to make new loans. As a result, credit was extended to local governments and government-owned entities to fund more new projects. While financing new public projects may be beneficial and perfectly well justified, we should consider that data indicating increased lending activities, implying a healthy economy, would include loans that were not necessarily issued in the ordinary course of business. Further, the Chinese banking system reportedly was faced with defaults and write-offs of a significant chunk of the newly extended loans, placing more pressure on the PBOC to deal with economic fallout.

That brings us to where we are today. The Western world—sometimes simply called *the West* and usually considered to include North America, Europe, Australia, and other developed countries—has been forced to deal with the export juggernaut that China has become. *Comparative advantage*, as discussed by Scottish economist Adam Smith in his famed 1776 book *The Wealth of Nations*, is imminently fair and good for the citizens of the world. It brings about his term *division of labor*, and over time accelerates and expands global trade, lifting living standards everywhere.

Sterilization is a different theme altogether. In fairness to China, it has been practiced by others in the course of history, including the United States, which sterilized in the 1920s and became supercompetitive. Our long-term trading partner and ally Great Britain, like most countries—including the United States—was on the gold standard then. Our cheaper goods, made so partially by sterilization, brought many pounds (British currency) into US banks. We promptly swapped them for their gold, leaving them no choice but to abandon the gold standard. We drained their gold vault and filled ours.

Although China is not the first to employ sterilization tactics, it has especially harmed its international trading partners because of the size and importance of the Chinese economy as well as the duration of its sterilization program. The buildup in foreign reserves, held in US currency as well as US Treasury securities, on the PBOC balance sheet is evidence of its prolific sterilization actions. But the explosive rate of accumulation of foreign reserves cannot be maintained indefinitely, as there are intrinsic costs to the banks that make it problematic. As long as the practice continues, the problem will grow in the form of mounting pressure on the banking system and the development of asset bubbles that may ultimately burst.

## COROLLARY EFFECTS

Obviously, for Americans, the most significant impact of China's monetary sterilization is the loss of manufacturing jobs. North Carolina's furniture industry is just one example of the devastation exchange-rate manipulation can cause. But it is more than just the management of exchange rates that does damage to China's trading partners, especially the United States.

China's sterilization practices result in the buildup of dollars in the PBOC's foreign-exchange reserve coffers. Because those dollars would otherwise just sit there, out of circulation, the PBOC deploys them into income-producing assets. And what better dollar-denominated assets are there than US Treasury securities? By purchasing Treasury bonds, the Chinese government is deploying otherwise stagnant reserves into income-producing securities that are backed by the US government. While the interest earned on the bonds serves to offset some of the cost of domestic sterilization bonds, purchasing US Treasury securities provides the PBOC with an additional means of control over the value of the dollar (strong demand for US Treasuries maintains their value and, thus, the value of the dollar itself). This helps to manage the yuan-to-dollar exchange rate.

The buildup in China's portfolio of US Treasury bonds can be clearly seen in data published by the US Department of the Treasury. While previously a significant player, China moved into the position of the largest foreign holder of US national debt in 2008. It is no coincidence that this shift occurred as the US economy went into a tailspin. Clearly, it was a measure by Chinese officials to help stabilize the value of the dollar in order to maintain the tight floating exchange rate with the yuan that allows China's export economy to flourish.

As the largest holder of US Treasury securities, China is in a powerful position with respect to the US economy. The Chinese government has accumulated a tremendous store of US dollar-denominated assets, and more are being purchased all the time. The longstanding trade imbalance has flooded the Chinese economy with US dollars that, through sterilization, make their way to the PBOC. Since we know that these dollars are used to purchase Treasury bonds, we understand that they find their way back into circulation in the United States.

They are being used to purchase bonds, which is just an asset swap. But the dollars represent current spending power that is being exchanged for future spending power. When those dollars come back into the US economy, they return that current spending power, which could be inflationary. Further, some assert that the monumental US national debt is evidence of reckless spending practices. Thus, the PBOC's hungry appetite for Treasury bonds encourages deficit spending, adding to the claim that China is harming the United States in myriad ways.

If comparative advantage and purchasing power parity were at work in the market, trade would swing back and forth more equally between the United States and China. Without the trade imbalance and monetary sterilization, there would be no one-sided buildup of foreign exchange reserves, and China would not be in a position to purchase such massive amounts of US national debt. It is just another example of the far-reaching impact of Communism, masquerading as free enterprise.

## SHADOW BANKS

Perhaps you've read about China's "shadow banks." While the portrayal of shadow banks as a sort of black market of the banking world is not altogether inaccurate, this secondary banking system need not be an enigma. Called shadow banks because they operate in the shadow of the commercial banking system, these lending houses emerged in response to the growing demand of Chinese citizens who were unable to borrow from traditional lenders. Basically operating without any sort of regulatory oversight, they often impose high interest rates, and the punishment for default reportedly goes well beyond foreclosure.

If the term *loan shark* comes to mind, it is because the shadow banks essentially operate in that fashion. While the connotation in America is that loan sharks lend to people who have bad credit or are skirting the law, it is not uncommon for average citizens to turn to shadow banks in China. Faced with onerous loan requirements and credit standards that prevent even the most creditworthy borrowers from obtaining loans, Chinese citizens are often unable to borrow from commercial banks. Historically, it was common in Chinese society to borrow from family members or close acquaintances in order to buy a home or expand a business. As the Chinese economy began its rise, human nature simply manifested itself in the desires of average citizens to improve their lives. The resulting need for credit became the driving force behind the emergence of the shadow banking world that we read about.

Nothing more than financial intermediaries, shadow banks work to bring those who have money to lend together with those who wish to borrow. The ability to create money out of thin air by the extension of new credit is a power that is unique to the commercial banking system. Since shadow banks are just facilitating the lending of funds from one party to another, they do not create new money by virtue of an accounting entry. They actually do lend deposits. So while new loans are made, there is no increase in the money supply.

While there is justified concern for the potential of fueling asset bubbles, the only real economic effect of the shadow banks is an increase in the velocity of the money already in circulation. Someone had money and lent it to another who is using it to buy a home or build a business. Rather than sit idle in an account or under a mattress, that money has changed hands and is circulating in the economy. This can drive productivity, but it does not increase the money supply. Therefore, it does not really impact the PBOC's efforts at currency sterilization.

## INFLATION OR APPRECIATION?

Although the foregoing discussion mentions that the PBOC pegs the yuan to the value of the dollar, that is no longer fully true. Under intense pressure from the West to let the yuan *float* (letting international markets through forex determine its value), in June of 2010 it began compromising somewhat by allowing the yuan to float upward in small increments within a range, over time. How this managed floating-rate system works exactly is not within the scope of this book, but it can be easily researched on the web. The important point is that when you hear US politicians screaming to

China to let the yuan float upward relative to the dollar, they are trying to eliminate the advantage of money manipulation.

Unfortunately, their focus is placed mostly on China's intervention in the foreign exchange market to influence the value of the yuan, hence the peg that was maintained for so long. Because there is so much confusion emanating from the misunderstanding between currency intervention and sterilization, it is poorly understood by most that sterilization is the larger problem. Because sterilization limits expansion of the monetary base and discourages growth, it has exploited the natural balance of trade and violated the law of comparative advantage.

China has maintained that its goal is to manage inflation. But moderate inflation would be a natural occurrence in an economy growing at the rate China has over the past few decades. So is their fear really too much inflation? Actually, prosperity drives up asset prices. Higher GDP pushes up the standard of living. Higher income creates higher values, but that is appreciation, not inflation. It is not only normal but essential to sustain a healthy private sector in a growing economy. By preventing a natural rate of inflation, or appreciation, from pushing the economy toward equilibrium, China's efforts have perpetuated a huge trade imbalance, resulting in predictions of banking crises and market bubbles that will ultimately burst. Further, China's private sector is continually suppressed, preventing improvements in the standard of living that Chinese citizens are earning by way of their productivity, yet are being denied due to government intervention.

Rapid, and arguably excessive, expansion in the export-driven economy has poured labor and other resources into that sector and prevented development of other areas of the domestic economy. Such is the cost of maintaining a supercompetitive edge in manufacturing relative to its trading partners. China's officials have pursued their overall goal of keeping the value of the yuan artificially low against the dollar in order to perpetuate the advantage of suppressed labor and manufacturing costs, keeping the cost of Chinese products cheaper and, therefore, more attractive. Basically, in macroeconomic terms, they have sought to bring about more real output with less M2 than the United States. They have successfully capitalized on this advantage for decades, but the inherent costs make their rate of sterilization unsustainable.

Perhaps we are already seeing signs of tapering in some of the shifts in monetary tactics and slowdowns in economic output. Although there has been pressure from the West and recessionary factors to deal with, the moves by the PBOC do seem to indicate that changes may be occurring. While China was not unique in dealing with economic recession in recent years, undoubtedly the environment in which the PBOC found itself was developed over years of currency manipulation and restricted growth, adding complication to the efforts to find resolution. Such is the way of Communism. It seems that among the most successful Communists are PBOC officials and Chinese exporters. Make no mistake: despite its recent changes to accommodate pressure from the developed world, namely the United States, China is neither a political nor economic friend and has no desire to become one.

# CHAPTER 7

## WORLD RESERVE CURRENCY

A discussion of how the money supply works both within the United States and around the globe should include an understanding of the status of the US dollar as the world's reserve currency. What does the term "reserve currency" mean? Why is it important? And how did the US dollar become the world's reserve currency?

## WHAT DOES "WORLD RESERVE CURRENCY" MEAN?

If you could travel back through history, you would see dominant currencies come and go in conjunction with the emergence and decline of world financial superpowers. Strictly speaking, a *reserve currency* is defined as one that is acceptable as a medium for settlement of international debts and is therefore is held in reserve in large quantities by many countries. To attain reserve status, a currency must be viewed as having a stable long-term value, and there must be a readily available supply of money and securities denominated in that currency. The US dollar satisfies both of these requirements.

The hallmarks of the dollar that make it especially suitable for this role are the strength of the US economy and the depth and liquidity of the US financial market. Despite its recent recessionary struggles, the US economy reigns as the largest and strongest in the world, lending confidence to those who store their value in dollar-denominated US Treasuries. Combined with the liquidity of Treasury securities and vast depth of the market (meaning that the market is relatively stable, as its size makes it less subject to the shifts in value that can result when a large amount of a particular security is bought or sold at once), that confidence makes the US dollar quite a safe bet.

As we dig into the benefits of reserve-currency status, let's consider what it means to the issuing country. It certainly sounds important. But the advantages of issuing the currency that the world holds in reserve go deeper than just bragging rights. Perhaps the most significant benefit, at least from a financial standpoint, is the ability to avoid transaction costs when trading abroad. Since the dollar is the standard, other countries generally must convert their currencies to dollars in order to do business with the United States.

Other currencies—such as the euro, the yen, and the yuan, among others—are sometimes accepted and used. But the dollar is universally accepted. For the United States, this eliminates the inherent exchange risk that other countries face in converting their currencies to dollars. Further, other countries are motivated to conduct their monetary policies in relation to the United States in an attempt to keep the value of their domestic currencies from straying too far from the dollar. This gives the United States the freedom to make policy decisions from a purely domestic standpoint, whereas leaders of other countries must operate within their own frameworks but still consider US policies in doing so. If their domestic currency weakens in relation to the dollar, they face the prospect of inflation. And if their currency appreciates, they naturally become concerned about their export sector (remember China?).

An issuer of reserve currency maintains more autonomy in going about its international transactions, enjoying the benefit of doing business in its own currency, with lower transaction costs. Add to that the lower borrowing costs derived as a result of other countries choosing to hold their dollar denominated reserves in the form of US Treasuries. This demand for Treasury bonds encourages stability in the US bond market. Along with that steady foreign demand for the securities comes downward pressure on bond yields, reducing the net cost of borrowing for the United States. While it may not be a direct effect, this is just another benefit of having the dollar accepted in most every country in the world.

## COSTS

We cannot examine the benefits of world reserve-currency status without asking whether there are drawbacks. One cannot attain any level of stature without some sort of cost. When other countries continue to purchase and hold US Treasury securities, yields are suppressed, which leads some to argue that the lower borrowing costs serve as incentive for the government to perpetuate its appetite for deficit spending. While we could argue the validity of the spending programs and the extent to which the borrowing costs actually influence the rate at which the government chooses to spend, suffice it to say that some economists consider this side effect of reserve-currency status a drawback.

Another downside of operating as a reserve-currency issuer is the resulting continual running of a trade deficit. As other countries purchase dollar-denominated assets, the United States runs an ongoing current account deficit, meaning that imports into the United States are outpacing exports to other countries. Is this a bad thing? Well, imports generally indicate that an economy is bringing in resources needed for production, while exports represent goods that have been produced for sale abroad. Dollars being sent overseas for purchase of imported goods are either held there in reserve or used by those foreign countries to invest in dollar-denominated assets. While increases in imports can signify production expansion, running a trade deficit for too long might lead to a buildup in foreign investment in US assets. The income paid to the foreign owners of those investments—whether Treasury securities, stocks in American companies, or real estate—would ship even more dollars overseas.

Typically, a country that runs a trade deficit also experiences higher national debt and, therefore, relatively slower growth. The buildup in debt is generally viewed as a drawback of reserve-currency status. Depending on the circumstances, it can be an inhibitor to growth. Consider, however, that the United States has been the world's reserve-currency issuer for decades, and the boom in economic growth that the nation has experienced over that time period is astounding. While the potential burden of world reserve-currency status may be unbearable for some, it is clearly not an obstacle for the United States.

With its ability to manage economic stresses by quickly adapting to changing conditions, the American financial system has proven time and again that it is strong and large enough to weather storms better than any other. As a case in point, action taken by the US government during the most recent recession, through its monetary policies, not only helped to stabilize the American banking system but also is attributed with dampening the recessionary impact to other countries. If the dollar's value had fallen drastically, the impact on the rest of the world would have been much greater.

Yes, the national debt has grown. And while one would expect to see a country with a strong, robust economy—one whose currency obtains reserve status—continually investing in other countries, the opposite may occur as time goes on. But we know that the US economy remains strong relative to others around the globe. Although there are those who worry that the net exporting of dollars may eventually erode that strength, we must not lose sight of the fact that the dollar has maintained its status as the standard for the world since the 1920s. It remains the world reserve currency for a reason. The world has confidence in the dollar as a store of value, and it trusts that American economic policies will lead the way into the future. The optimism and confidence inspired by America, derived from its democratic founding principles, makes it and the dollar uniquely suited to lead the world.

# THE RISE OF THE DOLLAR

So how did the dollar attain its status as the world reserve currency? Its ascension came naturally as the United States gained prominence in the world marketplace. Historically, dominant currencies shifted as different countries emerged as leaders of regional commerce. The British pound began a long reign as the reserve of choice in the 1800s as Great Britain became the world's largest manufacturer, leading in exports of finished goods and imports of raw materials.

At that time, most countries had begun to store gold in reserve. With the British pound being used for international trade and easily convertible into gold, its evolution as the world reserve currency was obvious. Moving into the 1900s, European countries like France and Germany became larger players in international trade, and their currencies became more prevalent, shifting prominence away from the British pound. Generally speaking, the period from 1915 to 1930 (the World War I era) marked the end of the pound's reign as world reserve currency and ushered in the rise of the US dollar. The transition was accelerated by the 1944 Bretton Woods Agreement, and it was solidified in the aftermath of World War II.

By the end of that war in 1945, most of the developed world, particularly Europe and Japan, lay physically decimated. The United States, on the other hand, had not suffered the destruction of battle on its mainland. Though the American economy had been converted from domestic production to wartime manufacturing (from cars to bombers), the country's industrial facilities and infrastructure were still intact. Companies simply pushed aside the tooling for guns and warplanes and pulled back the equipment sidelined in 1942, making a speedy return to domestic production. Sure, a 1946 Ford looked and operated just like a 1942 Ford, but at least there were new cars available fairly quickly. War-torn countries lay in rubble and thus faced a very different path to return to normal domestic production. The United States, through various rebuilding programs, aided former enemies in rebuilding their economies.

In full production mode, armed with new technologies learned during wartime manufacturing, the United States became an industrial behemoth with greater prominence in the world than ever before. Rapidly growing productivity allowed the nation to become a huge importer of goods. This demand for foreign goods and materials helped fuel the rebound for other countries' domestic economies. As these countries recovered and began exporting goods to the United States, they imported the dollars used as payment for these goods.

Those dollars were no more than demand notes, backed by the US government, to be used by these countries in the future. Would these dollars hold their face value over time? Could those dollar-holding countries redeem them for goods in the future? What was it about US dollars that gave foreign holders the confidence to accept all this paper? The Bretton Woods Agreement had established an international monetary system that fixed exchange rates to the US dollar and anchored currencies to gold. So, yes, the dollars were backed by a *gold standard*, meaning that a holder could, under that system (any new implementation of such a standard would likely not include redemption as an option), return the dollars to the United States and redeem them for gold. Was that enough to elevate the dollar to international reserve status?

The simple answer, of course, is no. The reason that other countries were, and arguably still are, happy to hold dollars as reserves against their own currency is that the dollars represented stable purchasing power. World War II had proven that the United States would, defying odds in the early years of the conflict, defend itself and its global friends against tyrannical war makers, whoever they were and from wherever they came. The United States and its allies ended the war with victory, and then the Americans extended a helping hand to assist in rebuilding the countries of former aggressors. This was done concurrently with the evolution of the nation into the most amazing peacetime lean-and-mean production machine in history. No one would dare bet against the United States.

The view of the United States as a strong, secure nation with a bright future carried over to the dollar, lending confidence in its value and stability. While it had already become an international means of transacting business, the worldwide acceptance of the dollar was solidified by the post–World War II boom, catapulting it into undisputable world reserve status.

## WILL THE DOLLAR FALL?

Will the dollar continue to reign supreme? This question is often the focus of news stories. To understand the variables involved, let's take a look at the following factors that typically distinguish a world reserve currency:

- *Availability:* There must be a significant amount of the currency in circulation around the globe, growing in quantity to meet demand. If it is to be held in reserve internationally, there must be enough of the currency to satisfy the demand of the other countries that will hold it. It is simple supply and demand, really.

- *Growth:* The currency must generally be growing faster than others, which logically means that the country's GDP must be growing at a relatively faster rate.

- *Stability:* The currency must be highly liquid and stable. While foreign countries hold sizable stores of reserves in cash, many choose to hold income-producing securities denominated in the reserve currency. They must have confidence that the securities can be quickly converted into cash and will hold their value in a crisis. Market depth is important in maintaining stability because it prevents ripples in value when larger lots of the security are purchased or sold. US Treasury securities, in addition to being highly convertible, are viewed as one of the safest, most stable assets available.

- *Trade Deficit:* The country issuing the currency must export significant amounts of the currency in exchange for imported goods and services. In other words, a country whose currency operates as a world reserve is typically a net importer, running a trade deficit with the other large economies in the world.

That last bit about a trade deficit sounds worrisome because classic economics teaches us that an economy can only grow if it is a net exporter. And, indeed, when the United States was growing at the rate that established it as the world reserve currency, it often did lead the world in exports. But the flip side of the trade deficit (also known as the *current* account deficit) is the *capital* account surplus, which is the balance of dollar-denominated assets that other countries hold.

While a deficit is generally considered to be a bad thing, there are good points in this case. It is evidence that other countries are accumulating stores of our dollars. Those dollars enable them to purchase our exports, so it all works in tandem. While they also use the dollars to invest in American assets, remember that, since the dollar is the world reserve, other countries want to *hold* our currency or Treasury securities. They are not motivated to cash out their securities or exchange the currency for goods and services. The US economy has actually seen a net benefit of the trade deficit, as the inflow of goods and services from abroad has boosted our standard of living to the highest in the world. We have financed it to a great extent with credit, whether in the form of cash sitting in foreign banks or Treasury securities.

So, let's return to our question: is the dollar at risk of losing its status and strength as the world's reserve currency? The economic conditions in the country during what is called "the Great Recession of 2008" naturally bring worries to the forefront. Many economists argue that the euro may become the primary reserve currency. It is widely accepted in settlement of international trade, with the size of the Eurozone's economy supporting its rise. Others believe that China's rapidly growing economy will bring the yuan to the forefront. Despite the PBOC's strict control, the yuan is gaining acceptance and popularity, making it a world player.

There are several dominant reserve currencies, all held with respect and confidence. Rather than overtake the dollar, these currencies operate alongside it as a means of international exchange. While it is true that these currencies are held in a reserve basket of sorts, it is unlikely that any other currency will ever replace or be held in equal esteem to the dollar, at least psychologically.

So when you read articles that suggest other currencies are overtaking the dollar, inciting fear, recall that there is a difference in a currency being used to settle international payments and actually being held *in reserve*. The world benefits from the strength and security offered by the US government, and it would take a lasting, widespread loss of confidence to change that. So read carefully and remember that the United States is still the largest and most powerful economy in the world, and the long-standing status of the dollar as the premier world reserve currency is not likely to change anytime soon.

## WHAT ABOUT THE EURO?

The euro, as we know, is the currency now used by the eighteen Eurozone countries. While it does comprise a significant trading zone, the Eurozone does not present as a united front in other financial and political aspects. As previously mentioned, while the Eurozone's monetary policy is unified by the common currency and common central bank, its fiscal policy coordination is in shambles. Think about Germany and Greece.

It is highly unlikely that the union will ever garner the strength to overcome the challenges of fiscal disharmony. And while the member countries are some of the world's oldest, the European Union is quite young. Reserve currency status is generally attained by mature economies with some type of track record. Will other countries choose the euro over the dollar? Not likely.

## THE CHINESE YUAN/RENMINBI

China, despite its emergence as an economic powerhouse, is still a Communist country, with its central bank (PBOC) run by major Communist leaders. The PBOC is strong and rich in assets; the Chinese people, well, not so much. As is typical in Communist regimes, the Chinese government's economic policies result in the private sector being continually suppressed, which in turn means that the Chinese people simply cannot afford to purchase large quantities of goods from abroad. Add to that the fact that the Chinese government maintains tight restrictions on the types of assets its citizens are permitted to hold, only allowing them very small amounts of foreign currency. And let's not forget that China has long maintained its position as a net exporter. In fact, China continually runs a huge trade surplus with the United States, amassing a vast amount of dollars in reserve, and it does so very purposefully.

So would it flip a switch, suddenly deciding to let its currency appreciate to market rates, enabling its citizens to trade abroad and gobble up imports and thereby become a net exporter of yuan? Why would a country so heavily invested in its export business do that? We know that China's leaders would probably love to gain the prestige of becoming issuers of world reserve currency. But if other countries are not exporting large amounts of goods to China, those countries will have no way of obtaining yuan to hold in reserve. While China is without a doubt an economic superpower, second only to the United States, we cannot forget that it has a long history of currency manipulation and suppression of its private sector.

When America rose to become the world's economic leader, it was riding a wave of respect that was won through strength and might in the pursuit of world peace and justice. The American dream was an ideal to which much of the world aspired. We can argue that the dream is tarnished and that the world has lost some faith in it. Does that mean things are so fundamentally flawed that the world would turn to a country that operates in secrecy and manipulation? The PBOC's intervention in the foreign exchange markets at the expense of its trading partners should make others wary. Recall that one of the primary components of world reserve currency status is confidence in the currency's liquidity and stability. Would you trust China? I think I'll stick with the US dollar.

# PART TWO

## RELATED TOPICS

With so many varying opinions proffered, deciphering current economics can be a bit like the proverbial quandary of being unable to "see the forest for the trees." A well-written article or essay can leave us with a sense that we should rely on what the author is saying because he has presented it in such a neatly wrapped package. While that may be true with some topics, economics is one of those areas where well-expressed opinions can easily be mistaken for fact.

There are so many moving parts in an economy that, even with a good dose of basic understanding, it can be a daunting task to figure out what works and what doesn't, especially when extrapolating the impact of a micro idea on a macro level. Notable well-educated economic "experts" often disagree. It makes for good press, but it can also cloud the issue for those who just want to understand how things that affect daily life are expected to change.

If you sift through all the clutter, it becomes clear that if you can grasp basic accounting principles and use a little common sense, you can generally step back from the "trees" and see the "forest" for what it is. That was the inspiration for the first part of this book. The most powerful tool we can strive for is knowledge. By improving our understanding of economics as applied to our daily lives, we can make better decisions for ourselves and those around us.

As we touched on in the previous sections, confidence is perhaps the most important factor in a healthy economy. In chapter 1, we looked at three pillars: confidence, monetary policy, and fiscal policy. Monetary and fiscal-policy matters are often the subject of news stories and political debates. But confidence is seldom a topic of discussion. While we must have sound policies in place, confidence is the key to a robust and thriving economy. When the future is perceived to be solid, the economy moves forward with enthusiasm.

A lack of confidence translates into fear for the future. Businesses and consumers pull back, leading to stagnation and, if it continues long enough, recession. Although it attracts little attention, the impact of confidence is pervasive. As we move into Part Two, we must keep in mind that, while political and other considerations come into play when focusing on a particular sector of the economy, confidence remains the critical element for stability and growth.

Now that we've covered a framework for understanding economics, we can take a look at specific topics that affect us on a daily basis. This goes beyond making sense of the news. Ideally, we will be able to use the understanding of how things work in our world to anticipate the future and implement strategies. Simply put, we can become proactive instead of reactive.

To that end, we are going to take a deeper look at three specific areas. Each of us can identify in some fashion with real-estate values, oil prices, and the fluctuating value of gold. Unlike stocks and bonds, these three areas in particular represent things that almost all of us will deal with at some point in our lives. Even the most cash-oriented person who will never purchase a single share of stock will probably buy gas for his car. He will live somewhere, either renting or owning a home, so the value of that property will hold significance in his financial life. And he most likely will wear or give a piece of jewelry to a loved one.

You may wonder why only these three were chosen for discussion. In addition to being commonplace in our daily lives, each is unique in some way regarding value. While easily identifiable by the average person, each is often misunderstood in terms of economics, giving these three areas particular interest for inclusion in this book.

# CHAPTER 8

## REAL ESTATE: YOU CAN'T LIVE WITHOUT IT

By its very nature, real estate is different from any other kind of investment. No other physical or financial asset behaves quite like real property. The total value of all real estate in the United States is estimated at $40 trillion, almost three times our annual GDP. Real estate represents perhaps 20 percent of the value of all assets in the United States, making it critical to understand its role in the overall economy as well as our individual economic lives.

Whether a personal home or business property, real estate is the largest asset in value that most people own. We form emotional attachments to real estate as a result of life experiences and memories that are connected to particular buildings or land, and it is sometimes difficult to ignore that connection and take an objective approach to buying and selling property. Because we all live, work, and play in or on real estate every day, we have an understanding of it that is not necessarily characteristic of other investment categories.

But do we really understand the impact of real-estate values in the ups and downs of the economy? Of all the lost value in various asset categories during the 2008 recession, real estate perhaps suffered the most, with prolonged and far-reaching impact on people's lives. Our focus for discussion is to gain a better understanding of how real estate is valued, how its value changes over time, and how to think about it from a purely investment standpoint.

## VALUING A REAL PROPERTY INVESTMENT

For the average citizen, real-estate ownership means purchasing a home. Most of us will never become investors in commercial property. However, when we think of the way real property is valued, investment becomes an important concept. Because the guidelines for determining the fair market value of an investment property are based on objective measures, they can also be helpful when entering the market for a home. The basic skills that investors use will certainly benefit a buyer who is attempting to balance the needs of his or her family with budgetary constraints. Even if budget is not the primary focus, learning to think like an investor certainly cannot hurt when shopping for that dream home.

Valuation methodology as applied to income-producing real estate is well understood by most real property investors. The predominant method used to determine value for this type of property, the *income capitalization approach*, begins with one simple question: how much rent will it produce? Of course, an investor will want to look at other elements, such as the condition of the property, any anticipated extraordinary costs, possible zoning or regulatory changes, and other concerns that could impact the current or future value of the property. As with any investment, income and appreciation may be the two most important factors, but particularly with real estate, the starting point is typically its annual cash flow.

It should be noted that there are a number of methodologies available for property valuation. Capitalization of income is one of several methods used by valuation professionals and sophisticated investors. While others, such as *discounted cash flows*, are sometimes used, the capitalization of income approach is the most common, primarily due to its fundamental premise, which extrapolates a future market value from current operating income. It seems particularly well suited for valuing investment real estate.

Other methods are based on different lines of thought. The discounted cash flow method, for example, is calculated by developing projected cash-flow data and then discounting the future expected operating income back to the present to determine current value. If you are reviewing a report from a professional appraiser, note the method he or she used to determine and compare values. That will help you understand the thought process behind the results as well as determine the amount of weight you place upon the appraised value in making your own analysis.

If an investor is scouting for properties to purchase and hold, his starting point should be the *net operating income* (NOI). Basically, he wants to know how much cash flow will remain after payment of all annual operating expenses, but before debt service, capital improvements, or income taxes. For example, imagine that a commercial office building is for sale. The potential investor, in doing his due diligence, learns that the property produces annual gross rents of $100,000. In order to determine net operating income, the investor must convert this gross income to the amount left over after the expenses of operation are paid. If these expenses are $40,000 (property taxes, insurance, repairs, accounting costs, leasing costs, etc.), then the NOI is $60,000.

This is a handy benchmark, but it should be noted that NOI, as used in property valuation, would most likely begin with normalized income, which would adjust for any unusual variances in the gross rental income as well as factor in an adjustment for expected vacancies. Expenses would be normalized as well, adjusting for one-time payments or changes in the allocation of expenses between the landlord and tenant. For example, negotiations with a new tenant may result in the tenant assuming payment of the property taxes. If we determine that the $100,000 gross rental income is a good average and normalized expenses will be about $60,000, the resulting annual NOI is $40,000.

While the NOI for a particular property is quite useful as a quick way for an investor to measure performance, it does not tell the investor what he should expect to pay for the property. That is where the valuation comes in. Using the capitalization of income method, the NOI of $40,000 will be used with a *capitalization rate*, or *cap rate*, to develop a market sales price for this property. The cap rate is determined by the following formula:

$$\text{Cap Rate} = \frac{\text{Annual Operating Income (NOI)}}{\text{Value of Property (Cost)}}$$

In this example:

$$\text{Cap Rate} = \frac{\$40,000 \quad \text{NOI}}{\$500,000 \quad \text{Price of Building}} = 8\%$$

The cap rate is a handy tool for a potential investor to use in scouting the market. It is often used as a rule of thumb and can be particularly useful in spotting trends in a particular market category. For example, if apartment buildings are trading at around an 8 percent cap rate in the local market, an investor would be able to use the NOI of a potential investment to determine if the asking price is reasonable. If the market-cap rate suddenly begins dropping, the investor may wonder if a bubble in the apartment building market is brewing.

As useful as the cap rate is, however, it can be misleading if a user does not clearly understand its purpose and limitations. While it does provide a quick look at the potential for a property, it is not all-inclusive. It is simply a quick way to explain the relationship between NOI and market asking price, and it is useful in spotting trends in a particular market category. Cap-rate analysis is limited in that it provides a snapshot of the investment that can change at any time. And it is only as reliable as the data used to make the calculation. While it can be a remarkably accurate predictor of expected cash flow, especially when normalized data is used, an investor should consider whether a more in-depth analysis of the property's condition and cash flows might be in order.

The investor should consider all aspects of the investment, not just the picture painted by the net operating income. After all, investors should be looking toward future returns and potential for appreciation. The NOI could change based on any number of factors. Even if a property passes the cap rate test, the following additional facts should be considered:

- market saturation in the area (supply and demand imbalance)
- age of the building (major repairs needed)
- economic outlook for the local area (rising incomes produce rising rents, which increases values)
- economic outlook for the nation (remember 2008)
- other investment opportunities
- local demographics and anticipated growth
- creditworthiness (quality) of current or expected future tenants
- other factors specific to the property or area, such as new highways or business developments underway or potential for highway traffic to bypass the area with new roads being planned

Any of the above factors could significantly impact the market value of a property. In this example, is a $500,000 asking price reasonable for a building that currently produces an annual NOI of $40,000? Maybe. If we assume that all other factors listed above are perceived to have been satisfactorily met in the potential investor's analysis, what else is left for consideration?

## FINANCING CONSIDERATIONS

One big factor in determining the overall return on an investment, maybe the most important of all, is the interest rate. While it is easy to become caught up in the analysis of an investment property from an NOI or cap-rate point of view, an investor should not forget about net cash return. Unless it is a cash purchase, the investment will be financed. An investor must factor in the potential cost of borrowing as part of the overall picture, asking some important questions, including the following:

- What return should I receive from this building?
- How much down payment can I afford?
- How much bank financing will I need and at what rate?
- Will I need to refinance in the future?
- What are the lending terms that I must meet, such as loan-to-value ratio and personal net worth?
- What are the remaining terms of any current tenants' leases and how do they compare to others in the area?
- What can I expect the market to support when those tenants renew or the space is released?

A prudent investor will take a step back and investigate a potential investment from an objective standpoint, including all aspects of the property that may affect overall return.

## TAX CONSIDERATIONS

While most investors are not tax experts and do not aspire to be, it is helpful to understand a few simple concepts related to real-estate investments. While income-tax expense is not considered in determining market value for a particular property, taxes do impact net profit. As such, income-tax considerations may be a significant factor in an investor's analysis of a property. This is certainly not an all-inclusive list of tax concerns, nor is it meant to be. Each taxpayer's situation is different, making it impossible to determine the way that a particular tax provision will impact his or her return without reviewing the specific facts. For investors, it is best to have some general knowledge of the concepts but leave the more complex matters to a professional.

When it comes to rental real estate, probably the most often mentioned tax deduction is depreciation. This is a broad concept but, in general terms, it relates to the fact that property will age over time, with the value of the property decreasing in some respects as a result of that aging process. In recognition of this reduction in value, the cost of a building or a component of that building, furnishings, or any improvements is generally subject to depreciation rules. Basically, that means that the cost of those items is not deducted for tax purposes in the year of acquisition. Instead, deductions are spread over a specified number of years, and those annual deductions are taken against the income generated by the property. Although it is not an expense actually paid in the year to which it applies, it is a deduction on that year's tax return. While the actual calculations are probably best left to a tax professional, an investor should understand that certain expenses may not be fully deductible in the year in which they are paid, but instead are taken as installments over some period of years.

For real-estate investors, there are two types of tax with regard to rental properties. First of all, the *net taxable income* from operating rental property is generally subject to income tax at ordinary tax rates. While there are some detailed and complicated rules involved, this typically means that the income is reportable and taxable similarly to wages and other forms of compensation. The other type of tax that investors should be aware of is *capital gains tax*. This is the tax applicable to any gain realized on properties when they are sold. It is generally levied at a lower rate than the tax on ordinary income, making it a bit less painful for investors.

The US tax code imposes different tax treatment for certain activities. For rental-property owners, the passive activity rules can be particularly problematic. The rules, which apply to most any rental real-estate owner who is not actively managing the property on a daily basis, are quite complex. Basically, they provide that passive investors can only deduct losses from operation of a property to the extent that there are gains from that property. Because of the complexity of these rules, most rental-property owners find that it is well worth the cost of hiring a tax professional for navigation of the passive activity rules, as well as general tax preparation and planning.

## THE PERFECT STORM

If you read mainstream news publications, you'll see that many journalists have come to believe that rampant demand and the expanding money supply (M2) in the economy were the big factors in pushing real-estate values to unsustainable highs in the early to mid-2000s. The theory goes that the housing boom was largely a function of the Federal Reserve action in providing so much liquidity to the commercial banking system that real-estate values had to respond. However, if you understand the fundamentals of the modern banking system, you know that this simply is not the case.

The Fed's policies certainly played a role in the housing bubble. A low Fed funds rate permitted banks to lower interest rates on mortgage loans, reducing the cost of borrowing. This made mortgages more affordable and brought more borrowers to the table, which worked in concert with other market conditions to increase demand. Rising demand pushed up appraisal values and provided seemingly reliable collateral for loans. The market was bustling, and lenders began competing for business, advertising low mortgage rates and simplified paperwork. But the availability of lending alone cannot drive buyers into the market. Demand is not driven purely by availability of funds. Rather, there must be confidence in the economy and a belief that values will rise. So while the banking system facilitated the situation, there were other factors at play. Let's take a look at the dynamics of the crisis.

At the center of what was really a perfect storm was an unprecedented boom in real-estate values. The early to mid-2000s saw home prices skyrocket with double-digit growth in many areas. If you look at longer-term historical trends for housing prices, you will see a pattern of growth, but it is obvious that this spike was far from the norm. Why did this happen? Was it fueled by Wall Street greed, as is often proposed? Was it the result of loose monetary policy? Were lax lending policies at fault? Truthfully, all of those probably contributed.

We know that credit policies were significantly relaxed, partly in response to the government-backed push toward equality in housing opportunity and partly due to competition for profits that skewed the risk vs. reward models for some lenders. Enter the subprime mortgage packages that we've heard so much about. If borrowers with less than stellar credit were suddenly able to easily obtain mortgages, often with shockingly little documentation of assets or verification of income, would we have expected to see anything other than an increase in demand for home ownership? And don't we know that increases in demand put upward pressure on prices?

There have always been mortgage products for those with impaired credit. The subprime mortgage was not new in the early 2000s. But the prolific use of it was a new phenomenon. Typically, subprime borrowers would be subject to higher interest rates, larger down payments, and other loan features that would be characteristic of higher-risk mortgages. Some of the borrowing that took place during the bubble did include some risk-adjustment factors, but it was typically less than prudent, leaving lenders with precarious exposure to risk. And it was all based on inflated real-estate values.

Adding fuel to the fire was the commonplace view of home ownership as a right, not a privilege. It is part of the American dream, after all. This underlying belief has become part of the fabric of who we are as Americans, and while it may be perfectly well justified, it was almost unavoidable that it would influence the perspective of investors and average citizens alike. No one would fault those who were attempting to better their lives. The fault lay with lenders who failed to do their due diligence. In an effort to garner higher profits, they lowered their standards and began to compete more aggressively for customers.

In their defense, government agencies seemed to support this position, with Fannie Mae and others continuing to promote the vigorous lending activity. Although it appears quite reckless in hindsight, the financial industry was responding rationally to the conditions in the market. When the economy took a downturn in the early 2000s following the terrorist attacks of September 11, 2001, and the fallout of the "dotcom bubble," the Fed funds rate dropped to a record low of 1 percent. This kept lending, specifically in the housing market, relatively stable while other segments of the economy were suffering. As is typical when the stock market is in turmoil, investors fled to the safety of Treasury bonds. Yields were pushed down, providing less return for holders, so banks and investment firms sought opportunities for greater returns.

Typically, as we know, the risk that a particular investment offers rises along with the potential return. This situation was no different. With cheap money available, the demand for the larger returns provided by riskier investment vehicles increased. Financial firms responded by securitizing subprime mortgages, resulting in the market frenzy driven by the now-infamous mortgage-backed securities. In hindsight, we can see that the banks and financial firms were responding to investors' demand for return and increased appetite for risk. While it is tempting to blame the bankers, we must step back and understand that, even though they were acting less than prudently, they did so in response to market pressures and governmental policies. Yes, it ended badly. But it was market demand and loose lending policies, not sinister intent, that set the stage for the fall.

When you combine growing demand and ease of borrowing, you see a spike in the housing market that grabs the attention of many hopeful investors. Along with the suggestion that home ownership is a right comes the idea that housing is also an investment. Since most people view real estate as a more stable asset than the stock market, you can see how speculators tuned right in to what they saw as a ripe opportunity. New investors were coming to the table in droves as they bet on what they believed would be fast appreciation on a high-demand asset. Soon, there was almost a frenzy, as rental-property ownership and "house flipping" became more commonplace than ever before. All of this activity was fueled by easier borrowing, which in turn helped create more demand, which fed higher prices. It is easy to see how the cycle continued with very little consideration being given to the precarious nature of the entire buildup. Hence, the very fitting term *bubble.*

We all know what happened next. In 2007, the bubble burst, and the fallout was devastating to the real-estate industry. Most believed that it was a housing crisis created by a sudden decline in values. Really, it was the end of what was an unsustainable rate of appreciation, which was followed by panic that caused that appreciation to turn negative. The downturn would have had a much less widespread impact without the massive growth in debt that had fed the bubble. The panic was justified, in that loan-to-value ratios were higher than ever before, meaning that even small drops in collateral value would cause real concern. With higher aggregate household debt levels than ever before, the impact of the fallout was much more widespread than it might otherwise have been.

The effects of the credit crisis were far-reaching, and no industry was considered safe. A common joke around 2008 or 2009, although not really funny, was that the only folks thriving were bankruptcy attorneys. Unfortunately, there was truth behind it. Most everyone was affected by the recession. Unemployment spiked, and those who were employed became fearful of being laid off. Many were faced with wage reductions, and discretionary spending came to a screeching halt. Confidence in the economy faltered, contracting demand. Unemployment was on the rise, and the GDP began to stall. As incomes dropped, borrowers began to fall behind on loan payments. Now upside down because of home values that had fallen below outstanding loan principal balances, many loans went into default.

Banks, under pressure to meet capital ratio requirements in the face of falling loan portfolio and collateral values, began calling loans en masse, even loans that were considered current. As a result, banks became the bad guys in the eyes of many frightened investors. This fallout was reported as a failure of the government to regulate the banks, and it was often misunderstood by the media and the public. But at the end of the day, it was a de-leveraging process that resulted in perhaps the worst economic conditions many Americans can remember. There were more sellers than buyers in the market, and values entered a downward spiral. What went up came back down. Harkening back to the Great Depression—which many of us only know about from history books, yet it is generally the time we immediately think of when talking about economic disasters—what was initially termed a "balance-sheet recession" has now become known as the "Great Recession."

When it became evident that the banking system was caught in a credit crisis of epic proportions, emergency government intervention became unavoidable. While many were opposed to bailing out the banks, the alternative was to allow the banking system to fail. Although some banks might have weathered the storm, anyone who understands the banking system knows that it is a network of independent banks working in concert as the engine of the economy. Allowing portions of the network to collapse would have pushed the faltering economy further over the edge. By choosing to intervene, the government, through the Federal Reserve, propped up the banks' reserve accounts and helped stabilize their capital. It was not an effort to push money into the economy, as many believed, but an attempt to restore stability and ease the fear that had begun to permeate the entire economy.

In lending to banks and purchasing bad assets (worthless loans and mortgage-backed securities), the Federal Reserve's intention was to prevent bank failures, reduce stress from weak capital positions, strengthen liquidity, and improve overall balance-sheet health. The result, however, was far more widespread. With some perspective, we can now see that the end result of the Fed's action was to restore confidence in the banking system as a whole, and thereby, begin to plant the seeds of recovery.

## LEARNING FROM THE PAST

While the recession of the 2000s is simple enough to recognize in hindsight as a bubble that burst, there were many factors that came into play besides increases in demand and loose lending policies. Demand didn't just suddenly begin to grow in 2000. The spike that occurred was predated by a gradual buildup in demand that naturally occurred along with demographic and cultural changes in the country that were soon reflected in investment portfolios.

As Americans came to view housing as an investment—and indeed we often still see advertisements that tell us that our homes are our largest investments—the brokerage industry responded. Prior to the early 1980s, the real-estate market was not liquid. Each investment property was typically owned by a small group of investors or by an individual. Because it was more cumbersome, time-consuming, and costly to buy and sell properties this way, real estate was, as a category, less valuable than other forms of investment. Further, the risk of owning properties with limited liability protection made the endeavor less attractive for small investors. Cap rates in the 1970s hovered in the 10–12 percent range.

By the early 1980s, however, a popular real-estate ownership structure called a *limited partnership* had come into widespread usage. To simplify purchases and address risk exposure, a general partnership would be formed to own a small percentage of a property and manage it, with multiple limited partners providing equity financing in exchange for ownership interests. Although the limited partners had less input in the management of the property, the potential income and appreciation over time provided motivation for investment. Because of the ease of entry and lower transaction costs for the typical small investor, the appeal of real estate as a category grew, bringing new investors and money into the real-estate sector. With this new supply of dollars driving new demand, values of real property rose across the board.

This, of course, pushed cap rates down to a range close to 8–10 percent, ushering in the *real-estate investment trust* (REIT). Although REITs were passed into law in the 1960s during the Eisenhower administration, the unique ownership structure began to surge in popularity as tax laws and other changes combined to make them a choice entity in which to hold real estate. By the 1990s, REITs were not only somewhat tax-favored, they were being traded as shares on a somewhat more open market, similar to mutual funds or the stock market. All of this made real estate more valuable in general, lowering cap rates even further. By the early 2000s, cap rates were in the 5–7 percent range, setting the stage for the bubble that few saw coming.

Now, very little of the previous discussion of the housing bubble has addressed cap rates. While they wouldn't be a concern for home buyers, investors should have been evaluating potential purchases with some kind of analysis, and they most likely considered cap rates. If they did, they would have seen those rates dropping, which could have led to a belief that real-estate investments were relatively better opportunities than other possibilities, such as the stock market. If we take it a step further and look at the NOI, the low interest rates in place thanks to the Fed's monetary policy would entice even the most savvy investor. So while it's important to understand cap rates, investors also need to know how to use them in conjunction with other tools for analysis. We must remember that they are not all-inclusive. Common sense and a general understanding of the economy can be as valuable as any rule of thumb or investment tool.

## BACK TO THE FUTURE

In the earlier example of an 8 percent cap rate, $40,000 NOI, and $500,000 value for the building, we were saying that an 8 percent cap rate is a reasonable return for that property in that current interest-rate environment. If banks were lending at a rate of 5 percent, for example, an owner could enjoy a 3 percent profit on the difference in the NOI (8 percent) and the cost of financing (5 percent), often called *the spread*, plus anticipated appreciation of the property over time. Assuming the investor is satisfied with all aspects of the property and it meets or exceeds his requirements, this may seem like a good investment. But what if the NOI is slightly inflated? What if significant expenses were overlooked? Certainly the cap rate would change. If the investor is using that as the primary tool for making his investment decisions, he might face a very different outcome than expected.

Based on what we know from the Great Recession, what should a buyer consider in addition to cap rates? Unless you know that the market is stable or that this particular property is exceptionally well priced, you might take a step back and look at the overall real-estate environment. Is there a possibility that you could fall victim to a bubble? Is the lending agency sound? Could you withstand the possibility of a change in your lending package, such as having the loan called if the value of the property drops in the future? With the recent crisis fresh in our memory, we should take some lessons and apply them in such a way as to become wiser investors. There will always be surprises, but we can use the new understanding gained from the nation's recent painful experiences to frame our perspective on new investments in such a way as to mitigate risk as well as maximize returns.

So what is the market-correct cap rate that an investor should seek? Is there such a thing? While it may be something different for one investor than another, there is typically a general idea of what a good cap rate is for a particular investment category. In 2014 in the United States, however, who knows? So how can cap rate be used for weighing investment opportunities? It is just the result of a formula that really means nothing if it isn't being used to compare multiple options. When considering real-estate investments, there are more variables involved than just cap rates. A prudent beginning investor would want to compare the potential investment properties to a standard. Remember that the cap rate does not factor in the cost of financing. It is really an indicator of the expected return on a cash investment.

Let's assume that we have a fixed sum to invest. Returning to our previous example, assume that we are looking for a way to invest $500,000. Treasury securities are often viewed as a standard for safe investments, making the Treasury bond rate a safe benchmark that is commonly employed when valuing other asset categories, including real estate. If we assume, for purposes of our example, that the current twenty-year Treasury bond rate is around 3.3 percent, we can use that as a reference point in our cap-rate analysis. Since our example analysis produced a cap rate of 8 percent, we can subtract the 3.3 percent risk-free Treasury rate from the 8 percent, resulting in a 4.7 percent risk premium. Then, when we look at the other underlying fundamentals of the property in question, we can decide if the investment justifies the additional 4.7 percent risk. Thinking about it in this way sometimes makes it easier to step back and view potential investments more objectively.

The market must take many variables into account when determining future real-estate values. Land and buildings only have value if people have a want and a need for them. That brings into the equation the word *demographics*, which turns our thinking to the population of the country as well as trends in housing and real-estate development. How many people? How much do they earn? Where do they want to live? These factors drive real-estate prices.

Demographers know that an important economic indicator is the *replacement rate*. Strongly tied to the fertility rate, the replacement rate is the number of individuals that must be born to replace those leaving this world. About 2.1 is considered to be the replacement rate necessary to maintain a stable US population. Everyone dies, but not everyone reproduces. For each generation to replace itself, each female must bear roughly 2.1 children in order to replace herself and her partner and to account for those who either do not survive to childbearing age or do not reproduce.

In 2013, the actual fertility rate was only 1.9, reflecting a lower birthrate during harsh economic times. Is the drop due only to economic pressures? Probably not, although recent history indicates that the fertility rate may decrease when confidence in the economic future falters. Does it automatically signify a diminishing US population for the future? Certainly not. Rapid immigration makes up the difference. The US Census Bureau estimates that by 2050, the United States will have a population of about 400 million people, up from around 300 million in 2010. More people need more developed real estate on which to live, work, and play.

Current housing-market trends show strong growth in urban areas. Job markets are changing, and more people now work from home or in virtual offices where they telecommute and teleconference. This has opened up opportunities for young, tech-savvy people to choose where they live, and they seem drawn together by the social and cultural opportunities offered in urban settings. That sense of community is a demographic indicator that many real-estate investors are watching. Patterns indicate a return to urban lifestyles, with the term *new urbanism* often heard in the context of mixed-use development and so-called "live, work, play" communities. This should certainly inspire a shift in demand and changes in value as interest in suburban living wanes and young people gravitate toward cities and towns.

While housing trends led by younger generations are certainly important, we must also consider our graying population. People are living longer, and so the housing choices of the older class demand attention. A growing trend indicates that many seniors are opting to relocate to urban communities, driven by a desire for a low-maintenance lifestyle, convenient access to necessary amenities like supermarkets and drugstores, and proximity to medical care. Senior housing communities are popping up as the market responds to the needs of this segment of the population.

What role does the real-estate market play in the national economy? Clearly it represents a large chunk of the GDP. Housing, whether individual or multifamily, plays the largest role, although commercial real estate is certainly not insignificant. Because GDP is an overall measure of the value of the nation's production of goods and services, it takes into account all of the activity generated by the real-estate industry. This includes the construction sector as well as real-estate-related consumption of goods and services.

The percentage of GDP represented by real-estate construction, both commercial and residential, varies in response to economic conditions. In 2006, it peaked at 8.9 percent, reflecting the boom in the housing market. As the crisis unfolded, the fallout of the housing crisis became particularly evident when the construction industry logged in at a painfully low 4.9 percent of GDP in 2010. While the measures show fluctuations in construction-related activity, the impact is felt beyond the construction industry. Real-estate construction has a trickle-down effect that is felt throughout the economy. Housing especially is linked to the unemployment rate and consumer spending, and it certainly is impacted by lending conditions. While we might think of real estate as a market unto itself, it plays a significant role in the nation's GDP and is a particularly sensitive measure of overall economic health.

We are a hopeful nation, and it is difficult to keep us down. Perhaps that optimism played a part in the perfect storm by flavoring the environment with too much expectation for appreciation. But it is also the key to recovery. We all know that economic booms and busts are part of life, and most of us are hopeful about the future. We learn from our mistakes and hope not to repeat them.

The pain of our lessons sometimes helps us to look at the things we understand to be true yet find new ways of thinking about them going forward.

We know that real estate and GDP are inextricably linked. We know that economic factors like unemployment and lending rates are important in gauging anticipated movement in real-estate values. We look to Treasury securities as a benchmark rate for measuring real-estate investment but attempt to also consider political and economic factors that may impact the bond market. Perhaps most importantly of all, we strive to gauge overall confidence in the economy. Increasing our knowledge of the way the economy works can help us to see the big picture, perhaps providing better insight into market trends. By learning from the past, we can direct our eye to the future of real-estate investment with an improved understanding of the markets and, hopefully, a solid foundation upon which to build.

Successful real-estate investors well understand the triple benefits of inflation, appreciation, and leverage. When the Fed wants to induce moderate inflation into the general economy, it reduces the target Fed funds rate to encourage borrowing and drive economic growth. People borrow to invest, and also begin shifting assets, in a search for greater yield. This lifts real-estate values, the obvious friend to a real-estate investor. Atop that, a profitable investment property that is based on sound fundamentals like location and condition may experience real appreciation in value. When combined with leverage, where a significant amount of the purchase price of the property is financed with beneficial interest rate and term, the growing value of the asset relative to the capital investment may compound that capital rather quickly. When you add the opportunities for tax deferral available under certain sections of the US tax code, the ability to compound capital is further enhanced.

Many great real-estate fortunes have been built on these principles. But beware—when the economy becomes overheated, either generally or in response to an asset bubble mode, the Fed will tighten and drive up the Fed funds rate. Credit becomes very expensive, if it is available at all, and that triple benefit becomes a triple negative. That ends a credit bubble, and this cycle has repeated occasionally in our modern times. The Great Recession of 2008 was an example of this, though it was more complex and severe, and the collapse in collateral values destroyed bank assets and, thus, capital. When real-estate values climb faster than real GDP, at some point, but inevitably, those values must correct, downwardly and painfully.

# CHAPTER 9

## OIL

Each and every one of us is affected by oil prices every day, whether we are purchasing gas at the pump, heating our homes, or buying vegetables at the grocery store. Energy is literally what makes the world work. It is pervasive in our lives, impacting almost everything we do. The price of anything that is manufactured, transported, or eaten is affected by changes in oil prices. And yet, the price of energy, oil in particular, is perhaps one of the most misunderstood concepts in economics. Because of the magnitude of oil's value to our economy and because it's such a part of our everyday lives, we should be particularly interested in understanding the way it is priced.

The pricing of oil, and particularly gas at the pump, seems complex, creating confusion for many consumers. Why are fuel prices so high? Do oil speculators manipulate prices, or are prices determined simply by the laws of supply and demand? What does the future hold? A shift in oil production and consumption around the world can have a profound effect on the entire global economy.

For example, the industrial and economic growth in China in recent years naturally resulted in an increase in the country's oil consumption, with a new demand for oil needed to heat factories and fuel manufacturing equipment translating into higher prices around the globe. While that is simple enough to understand, many wonder why prices continually rise faster than normal inflation over time, even when demand seems to stabilize.

## GAS PRICES DECONSTRUCTED

We're all familiar with the pain at the pump. High gas prices, fueled by the price of crude oil, are a constant concern for Americans. We are a society of automobile lovers, and whether we're working, playing, or both, we enjoy our cars. Unless you live in an urban area and can rely on walking and public transportation for your daily commute, you are well-acquainted with the budgetary impact of powering your vehicle. For those who travel by air, the cost of a flight is directly dependent on oil prices. The prices we pay for the goods we buy have transportation and delivery costs factored in. No one is immune to gas prices. Yet most people cannot really explain the breakdown of the cost of a gallon of gasoline (or diesel fuel).

There are five main components to the cost of fuel:

1. Cost of crude oil
2. Cost of refinement plus related profits
3. Cost of distribution and marketing plus related profits
4. Cost of storage
5. Taxes

While there are occasional manufacturing or refinement hiccups, generally speaking, production and storage costs are fairly steady. Marketing and taxes are typically consistent. The factor that is routinely responsible for the swings in fuel price is the cost of crude oil. As we all know from watching the news, that cost can spike suddenly, and annual swings of 25 percent or more are not atypical. If there is a most volatile element to fuel prices, the price of crude oil is it. But what causes these spikes? Are they the result of supply and demand, or do they emanate from the activities of the oil speculators that we hear so much about? Let's take a look.

## FUNDAMENTALS: SUPPLY AND DEMAND

One of the most basic economic fundamentals is the law of supply and demand. Given a constant supply of a good or service, an increase or decrease in demand for that good or service will push prices up or down. If demand is constant, changes in supply will result in either increasing or decreasing prices. While that rule of thumb is applicable in some capacity to most any market, there are those who believe that pricing in energy markets is controlled by more than fundamental economic factors. Regardless of any other influences, the facts show that the law of supply and demand is at work in the oil market. In fact, the typical annual swings in price can be related directly to seasonal shifts in supply and demand.

For example, we know that gas prices in America tend to rise each year around Memorial Day. It is no coincidence that this is the beginning of the summer travel and vacation season. Prices at the pump are higher in summer months because demand for fuel peaks during warmer weather. In addition to increased fuel demand due to vacation travel, some industries, such as construction and tourism, are busier during the warmer seasons of the year. Although winter weather brings with it a higher demand for heating oil, the combined effect of business and personal travel in summer results in a big increase in baseline demand. With a relatively constant supply, the fluctuations in price primarily result from seasonal changes in demand.

While there is a bit of variation, one particular aspect of the oil market that is different from others is constant, fixed demand. Because fuel is a factor across the board and plays some role in bringing almost every product to market, there is a certain amount of consumption that will remain regardless of price fluctuations. Because of this fixed, baseline amount of demand, there is very limited price elasticity in the oil market. Where demand in some industries is highly sensitive to price, fuel sales will not shift as much as a result of a price change.

Consider what would happen if the cost of a movie ticket began to increase. The number of moviegoers would decrease as the price ramped upward. At a certain point, maybe thirty or forty dollars per ticket, theaters would sit empty on Friday evenings. Other than movie reviewers, no one needs to go to a movie. The very few patrons who could afford to go and would pay the higher price to see a movie would be insufficient to sustain the cost of keeping theaters in operation.

Going to the movies is a choice, and consumers can opt out of the market. Compare that to the oil market, where only a portion of demand stems from choice. If you must drive to work, you will purchase fuel. If you must heat your home, especially if you are somewhere in the Northeast in winter, you will use heating oil. You may opt to skip weekend trips to the mall or set your thermostat to maintain a cooler temperature, but you cannot avoid purchasing at least some fuel, regardless of price.

The oil market has arguably one of the least elastic demand curves relative to price, and the industry is well aware of typical consumption patterns. If the industry constantly monitors consumption and seasonal demand is somewhat predictable, why are there unexpected spikes, and why did the price of oil increase drastically during the mid-2000s? The other side of the equation is supply. Generally speaking, under normal conditions, the oil industry has a relatively inelastic supply curve. The industry operates in such a way as to meet the demand of the economy with an eye toward maximization of profit. If all goes as intended, the economy is happy as consumers are satisfied and the industry hits the sweet spot in regard to profit. Oil tends to flow as needed based on industry experience with a reasonable amount of storage factored in as part of the supply-chain management.

Suppliers are tuned in to the market and know when it is time to tap new wells. When oil begins to flow, pumping generally continues uninterrupted until producers determine that it is economically beneficial to cap the well. There are routine supply shifts, such as in springtime when refineries temporarily shut down for annual maintenance and to shift over to production of summer-grade fuel, which burns in a cleaner and more efficient way, is kinder to the environment, and helps offset some of the spike in consumption during summer months. Because this timing typically correlates with the beginning of peak travel season, the impact of the interruption is anticipated, and the cost is absorbed in the typical summer price increase.

However, not all changes in supply are predictable or expected. Natural disasters, such as the hurricane that hit the Gulf of Mexico in 2005, can affect refinery operations and disrupt supply. Political unrest in oil-producing regions of the Middle East always creates uncertainty in regard to oil supply, so we generally expect prices to rise along with those news reports. Fear of disruption alone can lead the market to anticipate higher prices.

Further, the value of the dollar relative to other world currencies can play into the price of oil, which is priced internationally in dollars. When the dollar is strong against a basket of currencies, demand for oil in other countries drops, as oil becomes more expensive for them. As demand drops, the price falls. Conversely, if the value of the dollar drops, the price of oil rises as demand returns in those other countries. Still, all those price spikes are typically explainable and somewhat short-lived, and questions remain when we see fuel prices change, sometimes significantly, seemingly at random. If it is all supply and demand at work, why do we hear about price-gouging at the pump? And why is there so much talk about oil speculators?

## IS IT SPECULATION?

What is oil speculation? If news reports are to be believed, there is a concerted effort to influence the oil market by an exceptionally greedy lot of investors who trade in the oil markets in order to make a quick profit with no regard to the fact that, in the process, they are running up fuel prices at the expense of the average consumer. Is that what happens?

Simply stated, speculation is the purchase of an oil-related asset by a party who is anticipating a rise in the price of the asset, which will produce a capital gain on his investment. Some of those who speculate on oil prices are indeed investors, and they are only in it for profit, with no intention of ever taking delivery of a single drop of oil. Others who enter the market have a vested interest in fuel prices for business purposes and are looking to hedge—such as an airline attempting to control fuel costs. Finally, there are some speculators who may in fact be willing to purchase oil. While the motivations and intentions of those participating in the speculation market may be different, the mechanics are somewhat similar.

Oil speculation as a profitable activity has actually been around for a long time. As a practice, however, it gained popularity among investors outside the oil industry when derivatives products became easily traded on the open market. It stands to reason, then, that the rise in popularity brought with it an increase in journalistic scrutiny, making oil futures an often investigated editorial topic. While journalists' opinions seem to fall either solidly for or against the futures market's impact on oil prices, most articles offer editorial rants without really explaining the facts, perpetuating confusion and suspicion around this sensitive issue.

## FACTS ABOUT FUTURES

Futures contracts fall under the umbrella of derivatives products, meaning that they derive their value from the underlying product itself. While there are other types of derivatives, we are going to focus on futures contracts for our discussion of oil speculation, as they are arguably the most popular oil-related investments and also the most maligned. In the case of oil futures, the value of the contract changes relative to the value of crude oil. The terms of the agreement dictate the purchase and sale of a particular lot of crude oil, typically one thousand barrels, on a stated future date, at a stated price, with delivery to a particular refinery.

Traders are motivated to enter into the contracts, whether or not they actually plan to purchase or sell the oil, in order to capitalize on the volatility in the futures market. Basically, if a buyer believes the price of oil is going up, he may want to lock in at a price that is higher than current or spot prices but lower than where he thinks oil will be trading on the maturity date. For a seller, perhaps an oil producer, the reverse is true, with the intention being to lock in at a price above where he expects crude to trade in the future.

Futures contracts are traded on exchanges and settled through a clearinghouse, making it fairly easy for market participants to execute trades efficiently. Just as with most other commodities futures, contracts turn over many times prior to their actual maturity date, with each seller along the way hoping to make a marginal profit. Rarely does the initial purchaser hold the contract until expiry. The final holder has the option of taking delivery of the oil at the contract price, typically via delivery to a contractually specified refinery, or he can offset his position and accept a cash settlement for the difference between the stated contract price and the spot price on that date. As a matter of practice, it is quite rare, coming in around less than 2 percent, for futures traders to actually take possession of oil upon the maturity of a contract. The remaining 98 percent typically settle for cash, leaving the actual supply of oil untouched.

If the supply-and-demand equilibrium is largely unaffected, why do we see so many articles making the case that speculation drives oil prices up? A look at the mechanics makes it clear that the source of profits for traders is the purchase and sale of the contracts themselves. The futures market, unlike other commodity or equity markets, revolves purely around the trading of the paper contracts, with nothing being purchased upon entry into the market.

If you purchase stock, you are actually buying an asset that represents a share of a company. In the futures market, you simply make a deposit in a margin account, somewhat like an entry fee, which allows you to play. Then you enter into an agreement for a future purchase or sale of a commodity. You haven't actually purchased anything yet. Your margin account is adjusted as the value of the paper changes daily. You can trade your contract for another, taking a marginal profit or loss, or you can hold it until maturity, at which time you will most likely settle out by way of adjustment to your margin account. At no time during that process did you take ownership of any oil.

So how could you be blamed for causing an increase in the price of crude? In a sense, the futures market operates apart from and independently of the oil market. The two are linked because the futures trading prices are based on the price of crude and the value of the contracts will fluctuate along with crude, but the trading of futures contracts operates within its own system and responds to its own intrinsic forces of supply and demand. Unless the oil industry players are actually participating in the futures market itself, which they sometimes do to hedge against falling prices, they don't stand to incur any profit or loss from the trades. And unless speculators actually take delivery of the oil, store it, and remove it from the supply chain, they cannot affect the supply side of the market. As for the demand side, the fact that less than 2 percent of speculative contracts result in the holder taking delivery makes it pretty clear that the majority of speculators have no direct impact on the amount of crude on the market.

## TO STORE OR NOT TO STORE

So what about storage? If we contend that speculators can only affect oil prices by taking delivery of oil, can a group constituting less than 2 percent create enough of a supply-chain disruption to impact the price we pay at the pump? Should we fear oil hoarding by the market? While taking delivery actually entails ownership of oil that is physically being delivered to a stated refinery, at the end of the day, the speculator can dictate when that refined product hits the market. In the meantime, he must provide for physical storage of the product, either renting space from an oil company or dictating delivery to his own vessel. That is pretty impractical for a nonindustry speculator.

Whether in aboveground tanks or a fleet of ocean-borne tankers, oil storage is costly. It is a necessary part of the infrastructure for those in the industry, and we can be certain that they know exactly which levels to target for profit maximization. It would not be in their best interests to hoard oil in any significant fashion. And while the most cost-effective storage is in the ground, once a well begins flowing, it is economically disadvantageous to temporarily cap it in order to alter supply. So it is unlikely that an oil company will hoard oil, whether in tanks or by disrupting extraction processes.

Further, although oil-industry participants do speculate from time to time, most players are hedge funds and brokerage firms. They clearly would not be experts at oil storage, and the added cost would erode potential profits, making them less likely to accept the exposure for not only security but also environmental risks. While it can be marginally profitable on occasion for a speculator to arrange, in some way, for storage of oil, the associated costs and risks make it unlikely that it would remain a profitable long-term activity. We can surmise that for some, it may be an opportunistic endeavor, and they may get lucky on occasion, but the inherent risks of storing oil make it almost always a short-lived activity. As a long-term business model, oil storage is only practical for those in the industry.

## SPECULATION AND OIL PRICES

By addressing the impracticality of the storage issue, can we effectively dismiss the accusations of those who contend that oil speculators are directly responsible for price gouging at the pump? Not exactly. Speculation likely has influenced the crude-oil market, even pricing, in a small way. A few speculators do take delivery of oil, and they probably have some impact on supply and demand. While difficult to quantify, it is probably safe to say that the effect made by less than 2 percent of the volume of futures is largely insignificant.

Even if speculators suddenly decided to store an unusually and unexpectedly large volume of oil on a fleet of tankers, the impact of their decision would be temporary. Initially, prices would rise in response to the decrease in supply, but the market would shift over time as the industry gradually picked up production and covered the shortage. Then, assuming prices returned to equilibrium, the reintroduction of the stored oil into the market would ostensibly cause prices to decrease, returning to natural market levels.

Of course, that is market theory, and it would likely not happen that smoothly. The speculators would target the sale of their hoarded oil and attempt to enter it into the supply chain at a time when prices were peaking. The industry would likely react to the availability of that oil by adjusting supply, preventing prices from bottoming out so suddenly that consumers begin lining up at the pumps. Eventually, though, equilibrium would return and prices would settle out close to where they would otherwise have been all along, as ultimately determined by the interplay of supply and demand. The same scenario would be true if the oil producers themselves decided to restrict supply, only to release it to the market later. Eventually, natural market forces push prices back toward equilibrium.

All of this is correlated by the fact that oil inventories have remained relatively consistent. If there were huge profits to be had by hoarding oil, increases in inventory would be evident during times when oil prices peaked. Since there is no evidence of this happening, it is unlikely that there is a significant amount of storage manipulation in the market. While there may be some short-term impact on oil prices caused by the speculators who choose to take delivery of oil, it is unlikely that long-term prices are affected in any meaningful way.

## MARKET SIGNALS

What about the theory that momentum in the futures markets has an effect on the price of crude? The theory is that the issuance of an unusually large volume of contracts sends a signal to the oil industry that the market anticipates price movement in a certain direction. The contention is that oil producers respond to that message, particularly by hoarding oil with the intention of selling it later when prices are expected to be higher. The decreased supply would drive up current prices at the pump. Unlike an outside speculator who stores oil, industry insiders would have the power to control the overall oil supply.

If we stop there, it seems logical that speculators could be indirectly affecting prices at the gas pump. But we must consider that the oil industry can certainly not react overnight to fluctuations in the futures market—and that market fluctuates rapidly. A bubble could form simply based on euphoria in the futures market, driven by experienced and unsophisticated investors alike. What basis is there for oil-industry executives to gamble with profits based on bubbles that could pop without warning? That isn't to say that oil producers ignore market patterns. But oil companies are typically going to have the most accurate information about their own industry, and they will trust their own data over the reactions of speculative traders.

# BACK TO SUPPLY AND DEMAND

If speculation was not the driving force behind the rise in oil prices in the recent past, what was? To answer that question, we return to the rapid industrialization in China, India, and other emerging markets. Simply put, the world began to demand more oil. Supply, being largely inelastic, could not meet the overall global demand, so prices were pushed up and the available supplies went to the highest bidders. On a national level, the reduction in supply available to Americans resulted in rising fuel prices. We all saw it happen. We just didn't realize that it was the logical outcome of a shifting demand curve. In hindsight, we can see a classic example of the fundamentals of supply and demand at work in the market. The only way the oil industry could meet the sudden increased demand for oil coming from developing nations was to redirect some of the supply that would otherwise be available to everyone else.

Why did prices spike so much at a time when the economy was on the brink of recession? As we know, demand is not highly sensitive to price changes, so it takes quite an increase before we Americans will reduce our fuel consumption. Prices had to rise enough to cause consumers to take notice and adapt accordingly. Now, we know that the spike in oil prices leveled off and actually came back down. That is partially due to eventual production increases by the oil industry, but it also is attributable to the economic woes from the global recession, slowing growth and causing fuel demands to taper.

## PEAK OIL

If the law of supply and demand is the primary driver of oil prices, what would happen if we suddenly found out that the global supply of oil had reached its peak and would soon begin to contract? That very question is something economists are faced with as the scientific community continues to warn us of the finite nature of our oil supply. *Peak oil* is an industry term typically used to refer to the point at which an oil well, or an entire oil field, reaches its maximum rate of production. After peak oil is reached, the rate of production begins to decline until it is no longer economically feasible to extract oil from the well, or field, in question.

When we hear the term *peak oil* in the mainstream media, it is usually accompanied by dire warnings of the economic catastrophe believed to be looming in our oil-dependent future. As the theory goes, our global consumption of oil is moving at such a rapid pace that we are on target to run out of the resource in the near future. The idea of global catastrophe for our industrialized society is certainly attention-worthy, but where are the warnings coming from? Is there a scientific basis for concern, or is the peak oil theory nothing more than an attempt by the oil industry to support higher prices?

The theory of peak oil is not new. Coined by geoscientist M. King Hubbert in the 1950s,[6] the term suggests that oil production on a global scale follows a bell-shaped curve, similar to the pattern of production from a single oil well or field. Known as the Hubbert Curve, the graph illustrates that global oil production has increased on a gradual scale and will eventually reach a point of maximum production. After reaching this peak, the rate of production will begin to fall until it ultimately reaches a terminal point. When referencing the studies of Mr. Hubbert, the term *peak oil* refers to the point at which the world reaches its maximum oil productivity. From a scientific and economic standpoint, it not only refers to attaining peak productivity but also to the ensuing economic effects of the postpeak period.

And make no mistake, there would be economic effects. The suggestion that oil production has reached its maximum rate would set the stage for increasing energy prices, rationing of fuel, the expectation of hoarding, and probable security and defense challenges that would emerge along with fear of a future without fossil fuels. Economic confidence would nosedive, and the possibility of a global recession would set in. It is a perfect example of the law of supply and demand at work in the market.

This is no hypothetical scenario. The question is not *if* peak oil will be reached, but *when*. Science confirms that oil is a nonrenewable resource, as its formation requires specific geological circumstances and millions upon millions of years. There is no debate as to whether we will eventually run out of oil if we continue at our current rate of consumption. So why is there even a question as to the applicability of the peak oil theory? Since, in economic terms, peak oil is not about the certainty of whether we will eventually exhaust our stores of oil as much as the severity of the economic reaction to having hit the pinnacle of production and the fallout that will follow as supplies diminish, the debate revolves around attempts at answering critical questions like the following:

- What if we develop alternatives to oil as an energy resource, thereby reducing our dependence on fossil fuels?
- What if we improve our energy efficiency significantly, thereby decreasing our overall rate of consumption of oil?
- What if the point of peak oil is not a brief pinnacle but more of a plateau that lasts for a while?

Any of these factors, as well as many others, could alter the economic impact of reaching peak oil production. We might still see rising prices for crude, but that may have less effect on the broad economy if we are relying more on renewable energy sources like wind or solar power. Clearly, there is no debate as to the fact that oil stores can eventually be depleted. The impact that this has on us in terms of our economic stability is yet to be determined.

At the heart of the matter is the question of when we will reach the top of the bell curve. There are multiple theories addressing the timeframe for reaching peak oil, with some predicting that we will be there in the next ten years. Yet there are more questions than answers, and it is difficult to rely on any one study. Perhaps it is best if we do not know how long we have. If we fear that we are speeding toward imminent crisis, we will be more driven to find alternatives rather than pace ourselves as if we had time to spare. Adaptation generally occurs in response to necessity. We are not waiting for science to tell us the time for action is coming. We are frantically searching for new ways to tap otherwise unreachable oil resources.

Innovation, many believe, will produce alternatives that eliminate our reliance on oil as our primary fuel source altogether, thereby ending the economic crisis before it starts. So we may in fact never deplete the world's stores of oil. That's why some researchers debunk the applicability of peak oil theory altogether. Scientists are working every day to improve existing energy practices and develop new ones, leading most experts believe that peak oil production will not come as soon as previously forecast and that, when it does come, it will have far less economic impact than previously predicted. The key is to understand how the theory of peak oil applies in terms of economic impact. Then we can apply our understanding of the way the oil market works, based on the fundamentals of supply and demand, to guide us in making our own financial decisions.

## FUTURE DEMAND AND ALTERNATIVE ENERGY SOURCES

Projecting into the future, no one can say with certainty what fuel prices are expected to do. We know that world oil stores remain flush for now, and we are constantly coming up with new ways to tap into oil reserves. Typically, oil extraction reaches its maximum production when about 50 percent of the oil is pumped from a particular well. And wells are never completely exhausted. At some point, extraction reaches a point at which it is no longer economically advantageous to continue pumping and a well is capped. Thus there are substantial stores of oil that are effectively inaccessible. For many years, it has been more efficient to simply move on to the next source rather than find new ways to extract remaining oil from previously tapped wells.

Now, however, economic and political conditions are making

it a priority to develop methods of reaching these remaining stores of fossil fuel. Fracking, which involves extracting oil from shale, is probably the most well-known of these methods. Although it is controversial, it seems promising in terms of oil production. Much research is being focused on the environmental impacts of fracking, in hopes that it will be a developed into a viable alternative for the future of the industry.

If the price of oil had never increased, perhaps we would not be focused on alternative means of oil extraction. But we consumers are motivated by our wallets, and it is no surprise that we are now dedicating renewed efforts to finding alternative sources of energy. Whether it is fracking or another method of accessing oil reserves, we can assume that we will find a way to free up previously unreachable stores of fossil fuel. Still, there will come a time when the availability of oil becomes a concern. That is the catalyst for the race that is occurring within the scientific community to find alternative ways to power our world.

As with so many past dilemmas, we will surely innovate our way to a solution to our energy problems. Future generations will likely be far less dependent on oil. For now, however, we remain beholden to fossil fuels, making the price of crude an ongoing area of focus and fear. By understanding the true forces at work in the oil market, we hope that we can filter out the hype and make thoughtful and wise decisions in our own economic lives.

Our nation will also have to make thoughtful and wise decisions, and this is one of the central economic points of this chapter. As of 2014, the United States is a net importer of crude oil. We are also an exporter of refined product, as export of crude oil is forbidden under current law, although that is likely to be allowed in the near future. We use more crude than we produce domestically and approximately 40 percent of our total annual consumption must be derived from imports, equating to roughly $300 billion in real money. That means that we are essentially spending $300 billion with other countries in order to meet our need for crude. Experts calculate that the United States is well on its way, in the near-term future, to becoming a net exporter of oil products. Thus, the balance would shift and we would become a net importer of dollars from those sales.

It is beyond the scope of this book to estimate this volume or price, but what if, for example, we flipped from being a $300 billion importer of oil to a $300 billion exporter of oil—a $600 billion swing? That is a tremendous increase to our GDP. It is money that spreads wealth over all US citizens, including those in new jobs in the oil and gas industry. This is, to some degree, a game changer. It is evidence that man has developed technology to exploit what has been under our feet for millennia. This oil certainly lubricates and energizes our economy, and our free-enterprise system allows us to enjoy the benefits of our good fortune.

# CHAPTER 10

## GOLD: WHAT IS IT REALLY WORTH?

If you watch television at all, you've probably seen one of the commercials featuring a television personality who issues dire warnings that an economic collapse of epic proportions is imminent and advises viewers to protect themselves by buying gold. There are similar ads that surface on the Internet, often with video presentations making the case for gold as the only sure way to avoid economic disaster. Do these people really know something the rest of us do not? Common sense tells us the only reason these ads exist is because someone, aside from the actors being paid to get our attention, is making money from them. The videos are compelling, and fear is a powerful motivator. While a reasonably intelligent person can see through the hype, there is still much confusion about gold. To make sense of it, we must filter out emotion and present the facts in a framework that simplifies how we should think about gold.

Gold does not have much relevance in our daily lives. We could easily live without it. But gold has a mystique about it that makes it unique. We revere gold for its lasting sense of value and the weight it carries in our minds. No other tangible thing, metal or otherwise, has captured our imaginations through the ages the way gold has. In large part, this stems from the fact that gold once was a predominant form of money. It still is respected as a store of value because it is somewhat accepted as a medium of exchange. From a purely technical standpoint, that qualifies it as money. But while it is exchangeable into currency in the marketplace, it is not an efficient or practical form of money. It is quite bulky to carry around, and you can't exactly use it at the gas pump or the grocery store. Thus its lack of everyday relevance.

If gold is so impractical as money, why do we place it on such a high pedestal? Consider the images that come to mind when you think about gold. Most people envision gold bars, coins, or jewelry. Most of us have a ring or watch or some other piece made of gold, perhaps a beautiful heirloom passed down from previous generations. If you let your mind go back in time, visions of pirates with chests of gold coins come to mind. History books show pictures of Egyptian pharaohs with layers of ornate gold embellishments. As a culture, we are programmed to think of gold as valuable and lasting. And it does have lasting value. It never becomes obsolete. We would never just throw away a piece of gold like we do so many other things. That alone tells us that gold is a bit different from most other asset classes. We must think differently about it, separate feelings from facts, and take an objective look at its true value.

## VALUE AND CONFIDENCE

Let's start with some basic facts. Gold is almost impossible to oxidize or corrode. An atom of gold is always going to be an atom of gold. Separating the electrons from the nucleus of an atom of gold is more difficult to accomplish than for most other elements in the universe.

Gold can be melted and alloyed with other metals. That alloy can then be melted again and returned to its pure gold atomic form. This means any gold ever mined in the world's history is still with us, whether in an industrial or electrical device; a gold coin; a bar of gold in your safe-deposit box or at the Federal Reserve Bank's vault at Fort Knox, Kentucky; the filling in your tooth; a necklace around your neck; or the wedding band on your finger.

How much gold is there? If all the gold in the world was gathered, melted, and formed into a single cube, that cube would measure about sixty-seven feet per side. Interestingly, that represents a little less than one ounce per person in the world. Its worth? You could calculate it daily if you cared to, but on any given day, it would be worth about $10 trillion, give or take a trillion or so. That's a lot of money—equivalent to two-thirds or so of the annual GDP of the United States or about one-seventh of the world's GDP.

In trying to determine a rule of thumb for calculating the value of gold, another statistic worth noting is that over several decades, the price of gold has been roughly 3.4 times the Consumer Price Index (CPI). The CPI has been developed by the Bureau of Labor and Statistics of the US Department of Labor and used over several decades to measure annual inflation in the economy. The many details of this calculation are beyond the scope of this book, but the raw number of about 233 in August 2013 is appropriate to use for the following example:

| CPI | | Historical Multiplier for Gold | | Price of Gold |
|---|---|---|---|---|
| 233 | x | 3.4 | = | 792 |

This 792 is well below the typical price of an ounce of gold for the 2009–2013 period. In fact, gold traded as high as $1,800 per ounce during that period.

Why the spike in price? Fear! Clearly, the 2009–2013 period was wrought with economic stress and worry. Americans were concerned about financial stability and security, with many facing unemployment and displacement as jobs disappeared and homes went into foreclosure. Gallup's US Economic Confidence Index, which bases its measure on the perception of current economic conditions and whether the economy is getting better or worse, bottomed out in 2008. The Consumer Confidence Index (CCI), as measured by the Confidence Board, reported similar results, with the CCI reflecting dramatically low readings in the fourth quarter of 2008. Since the price of gold can be viewed as a barometer of confidence, it is no surprise that the gold market began a steady upward climb around that same time.

Gold trades primarily on fear rather than real economic fundamentals. When economic troubles arise and confidence is eroded, gold becomes a safe haven for those who believe that it has stable, intrinsic value. But does that make it a good investment? How should we look at gold as an asset class? Are there real reasons to include gold in an investment portfolio?

## GOLD AS AN INVESTMENT

Should we buy gold? Should a percentage of our savings be allocated to gold as a hedge against inflation? Let's consider that gold, as an asset, behaves differently than other classes of assets. It provides no real return or income. Yes, there are hedge funds based on gold positions, and you can consider the fact that gold may increase in value, thereby providing a gain if you sell it; but simply holding an amount of gold does not provide the purchaser with any immediate return. Thus, it behaves in a sense like the commodity that it is.

But while it fits the definition of a commodity, it does not behave typically in that category either. Because gold is also viewed as a form of money, its price is driven somewhat by the belief that it has a stable value. Further, there is confidence that the market for gold will always exist, eliminating the fear that plagues other commodities markets. The fact that gold can be exchanged into money with some expectation of reliability adds a premium to the value that it would otherwise hold. Since gold is not purely speculative in nature, many see it as a way to secure the value of their savings in an environment of economic uncertainty. And although the basic rules of supply and demand do come into play, the value of gold is also affected by psychological perceptions.

When inflation is anticipated and the value of the dollar is falling, gold prices tend to rise. Initially, this has nothing to do with the supply of gold. It is merely a reaction to the perceived loss of value of the dollar. Of course, when more people begin to come into the gold market, the increasing demand continues to drive the price upward. As previously mentioned, economic confidence bottomed out in 2008. Because of the severity of the recession and the fear that government stimulus actions, in the form of quantitative easing, would lead to inflation, gold began an upward run that lasted well into 2013, outperforming most other asset classes during that period. Clearly, this was a reaction to fear and uncertainty, not anything fundamental to the gold market itself. While those who bought gold may have profited, they did so only because Americans were paralyzed with fear and a lack of confidence in the future.

So what about those television commercials? They make it sound as if gold is the only way to ensure financial security. Certainly many of those who flocked to gold in its recent heyday did feel quite pessimistic about the future of the American economy. All of us were concerned about where the United States was headed, and even the world. But in terms of how we invest money and where we allocate our savings, we must remember to maintain balance. Investment advisors typically recommend diversification in a portfolio, with periodic rebalancing. Many advise that some income-producing stocks and a small percentage of cash be held along with a small position in gold or some other commodity as a hedge. But the majority of a typical investment portfolio is generally allocated to growth stocks.

What does this tell us? It's all about confidence! If you view growth stocks as a belief in the productive future of the economy, this translates as a belief in the American drive to grow and produce. It is basically a statement of confidence in the future. Those who advocate hoarding gold are banking on fear. They are buying into a pessimistic view of not only the economy but the overall spirit of the human race. They are gambling on the likelihood of the long-term economic failure of a country that has a history of invention, production, innovation, and success. They are promoting an idea that goes against the track record of the strongest country in the history of the world. Yes, there are economic downturns and, yes, there are political hurdles along the way. But buying into the "sky is falling" hype of those gold-peddling commercials is essentially making a bet that we will fail to overcome as we always have.

All of this makes it sound as if it is un-American to buy gold, as if we are defaulting on our patriotic duty if we buy into the belief that gold is the only way to stop the hemorrhaging in our portfolios. It really is not a political statement at all. Gold is not a bad thing to own; it is simply unproductive. It has some value as a commodity, and its use in certain sectors of manufacturing can be productive. But buying a bar of gold is not a true investment, and dumping large amounts of savings into gold as an inflation hedge is giving in to fear. Don't let the fear of economic collapse drive you to buy into the hype when history tells us that productivity and ingenuity are better long-term bets than bars of gold will ever be.

In truth, if a catastrophic event did occur, causing the economy to collapse and devaluing the dollar completely, the least practical thing anyone would trade for would be gold. What would they do with it? Who would accept it anyway? Most likely, we would be bartering food for weapons or other means of providing security amid the chaos, not gold coins or bars.

## THE GOLD STANDARD

Typically something that we hear referenced in sound bites around election time, the *gold standard* is defined by the Library of Economics and Liberty as a "commitment by participating countries to fix the prices of their domestic currencies in terms of a specified amount of gold."[7] If a country adheres to a gold standard, that country's currency, both national notes and bank deposits, could theoretically be redeemed at a specified price for gold. Throughout history, many countries, including the United States, have operated under a gold standard system at some time, although no country currently does so. Lacking a monetary system based on gold or any other resource, the US dollar now is known as a *fiat currency*, or money declared to be legal tender by the government but lacking intrinsic value.

Would a return to a gold standard stabilize the value of our currency—or any country's currency? Is it even possible? These are questions often posed in political and economic discussions. Some very noteworthy people are staunch supporters of the idea that the United States should return to a modified currency standard based on the price of gold. The basic premise is that the value of the dollar would be fixed to the value of a specific weight in gold. Essentially, the value of all goods and services would be measured based on the value of gold, with legal currency like the US dollar simply being used to represent that value. As with most things, there are strong opinions on both sides of the gold-standard argument and it can often be confusing.

Supporters argue that gold is an appropriate anchor of value because it is a nonrenewable resource with a fixed, known quantity. A policy equating dollars with a fixed weight of gold would thus stabilize the value of the dollar and other world currencies. An essential element of the gold standard is that the supply of dollars would be fixed to the value of gold. If the United States once again adopted a gold standard, the system would impose restraint on government spending, helping to curtail excessive behavior and move toward a balanced budget environment. For those who fear that government spending is speeding the United States down a path toward economic destruction, this sounds like a good plan.

But would returning to a gold standard solve the problem? It is true that a restrictive system would impose additional limits on the government's ability to spend. While that sounds like a good thing, those same restrictions would limit many actions of the government that most people find beneficial. These limitations built into the system were much of the reason that the United States, as well as other countries, moved away from the gold standard in the past. Such rigidity does not necessarily create good behavior any more than the mere existence of laws forces citizens to follow them. In fact, past failures under the gold standard were due in part to deficit spending and corruption. If the restrictive nature of the system did not prevent misbehavior in the past, why would anything be different now, in an age where most people believe the government to be wrought with corruption anyway?

In truth, the adoption of a gold standard would likely not change economic behavior that is baked into our belief system and our habits. It is naïve to think that such a conversion would automatically change political behavior. A country's monetary system is a product of the nation's citizens and their chosen leaders. If they were motivated to act a certain way, preferably honorably and for the overall good, they would do so under the fiat currency system that we have. If the system is broken or corrupt, it is due to the actions of those in leadership positions and the behavior of those who participate in the system with significant impact. At the end of the day, it all comes down to choices made by individuals, and we humans sometimes do not follow the rules. While the return to a gold standard might impose more restrictions on human behavior, it would not necessarily curtail the actions of those who are determined to ignore the rules.

How about economic security? Gold-standard proponents argue that economic bubbles can be avoided if there are controls on the rate of growth in the economy. Would that help avoid wild swings in values and prevent recessions? There may be less opportunity for bubbles, and perhaps the economy would grow at a more consistent pace. But that potential for predictability comes at a price. Any time you attempt to control growth, you also restrict flexibility. And we must remember that economic security is affected by more than inflation and inconsistent growth in values.

Where a fiat currency system provides flexibility that enables the issuing country to intervene in times of recession or national crisis, a country operating under a gold standard is held economically captive based on the value of gold. With a fiat currency, the government is able to step in and authorize new currency issues when necessary to mitigate recessionary trends, preventing fallout like price instability or government default. Where a sovereign currency issuer enjoys the benefits of floating exchange rates, a gold standard prevents government influence or interference, making a country operating at a trade deficit particularly vulnerable to recession. This most certainly would affect the United States and is one of the reasons that a return to a gold standard is unlikely.

Perhaps the biggest reason that the gold standard will likely remain a thing of the past, though, is the fact that it limits economic expansion and significantly curbs the ability of the government to react promptly with policy actions when needs arise. In times of crisis, such as national threats of terrorism or war, a government operating under a gold standard would be limited in its ability to provide the new capital needed to respond to sudden demands for defense equipment or technology. If the country was headed into recession, the government would be unable, under a gold standard, to immediately enact measures to prop up failing banks or preserve certain industries, leading to potentially disastrous economic consequences. While it should be noted that some advocates claim emergency-response powers could be built into a gold-based system, there would still be significant limitations on economic expansion.

The restrictions that are hailed as being the way to prevent economic bubbles would also limit what may be healthy and appropriate economic growth. In the modern technological age in which we live, industries change and new product lines spring up rapidly with innovation. Restricting the ability of certain sectors of the economy to adapt and grow could stunt GDP and the ability of the country to compete on a global, technological scale.

This is not to say that government spending should go unchecked or that there should not be a system of controls. But a nation cannot abdicate its responsibility to manage its monetary policy, or control choices made by its citizens, by tying its currency to gold. Good stewardship should be practiced regardless of the system being followed.

As is appropriate in a democracy, it comes down to the people.

Americans have the right to vote and should exercise that right faithfully and enthusiastically, placing those people in office who will serve as good stewards of the economy, making the best possible decisions for the good of all. Why anchor a currency to gold when gold's value is primarily based on emotion? Would you rather believe in the Fed making well-intentioned decisions, which only occasionally prove to be less than prudent, or the whims of the masses, who ultimately determine the price of gold at any given time?

## WHAT DOES THE FUTURE HOLD?

None of us can be certain how future events will unfold, but most believe that the fiat currency system is here to stay. The decision to abandon the gold standard in the United States was made deliberately. In the midst of the Great Depression, the US economy was failing miserably, driving many citizens to cash in their dollar-denominated deposits for gold. Americans had lost faith in the economy. President Franklin D. Roosevelt's decision to cut the dollar's tie to gold in 1933 enabled Congress to inject money into the system, lowering interest rates and restoring economic confidence. The move is credited by many economists as the single most important act to bring the country out of depression. Yes, some ties to gold remained until the 1970s, but the gold standard had been abandoned and hindsight validates that the decision paved the way for prosperity.

Americans tend to move forward with optimism, ideally learning from our mistakes and making better choices in the future. Gold is many things—a beautiful metal, an excellent conductor, a vintage heirloom, a store of value—but it is not a foolproof investment. It is a commodity whose value is determined not by pure fundamentals like supply and demand but by reference to its perceived worth as money and by psychological factors like fear and uncertainty. To reinforce that gold is only worth what people think it's worth and has little utility in the real world, we can look to the guidance of a pretty successful investor from Nebraska, a fellow named Warren Buffett. Here are two of his well-known sayings on gold:

> Gold is a way of going long on fear, and it has been a pretty good way of going long on fear from time to time. But you really have to hope people become more afraid in a year or two years than they are now. And if they become more afraid you make money, if they become less afraid you lose money, but the gold itself doesn't produce anything.

> [Gold] gets dug out of the ground in Africa, or someplace. Then we melt it down, dig another hole, bury it again and pay people to stand around guarding it. It has no utility. Anyone watching from Mars would be scratching their head.[8]

Common sense at its best.

# CONCLUSION

*Money is only a tool. It will take you wherever you wish,*
*but it will not replace you as the driver.*
*—Ayn Rand* [9]

Money represents many things to many people. What is a resource for some can be a burden to others. Many people make money a goal, doing whatever they can to obtain what they envision as the ultimate status symbol. Others strive to live simply, taking a view of money as a necessary means of survival but little else. The majority of people fall somewhere in between, desiring enough wealth to provide security and peace of mind plus a cushion beyond that which allows them to partake in a few luxuries and indulgences.

For economists—and perhaps now the reader who has completed this journey through the nuts and bolts of the economy—money is most definitely a tool. The product of the banking system, it is the essential element that fuels everything else in the economic engine. Money is created endogenously within the private sector by virtue of the commercial banking system's loan creation process. Perhaps that is the single most important nugget to take away from this book: the way the banking system works.

Whether you are an aspiring economist, a young business

professional, a hopeful entrepreneur, or just an average citizen who wants to better understand the world we live in, you will certainly benefit from having insight into how the credit-creation process works. You will be a better investor if you can navigate the way the commercial banking system works in conjunction with the Federal Reserve and the Treasury and anticipate how their interplay will impact the markets. You will be a more informed voter if you understand the role that government plays in influencing the money supply, helping you to evaluate political candidates and their platforms without being swayed by sound bites and fear tactics. You will be a more astute consumer if you are able to understand market cycles and the factors that influence supply and demand. All of these things combine to make you a better citizen.

Understanding the economy does not need to be an arduous task. It really is quite simple. Economics is not pure science. It involves a healthy dose of psychology. Predicting reactions and motives of others is fundamental to seeing the whole picture. For most of the countries that are part of the global economy, it is as much about feelings and human nature as it is about business and government. At its most basic, it is about confidence; it is about unleashing our animal spirits, as economists like to say. That is as it should be in a free-market economy that is the hallmark of a capitalist system and a democratic society such as we have in the United States. Money is just a tool. The driver is the human spirit.

That brings us to the end of our economic journey. I hope that you have learned a few things and that you are inspired to continue to learn. Each of us is a part of the global economy, and each of us has a right to understand what makes it tick. Cyndi

Lauper sang that "money changes everything." I think knowledge changes everything, and I hope that this book has helped you gain confidence in your understanding of the way our world works.

In considering the balance between the public and private sectors and the equilibrium of the three pillars of the economy, I smile and recall an acronym that was introduced to me in MBA school. It was on the first day of a class taught by a PhD economist we students all feared for his brilliance. I remember it well. It was an economic decision-making and analysis class, and we expected high-level math and all kinds of complicated formulas.

The professor walked to the chalkboard (we still used chalk back then) and said, "I am going to write something on this board that is going to be the heart and center of my course for the entire semester." As we watched, he wrote the following letters in all caps:

TANSTAAFL

At the time, very few people had heard of that acronym, so we were all watching in fear and anticipation as he looked at us, grinned, and wrote under the letters, "There ain't no such thing as a free lunch." We all laughed with relief.

# SUGGESTED READING

- For further reading about the structure, operation, and makeup of the US Federal Reserve, visit http://www.FederalReserve.gov.
- For further reading about the operation and duties of the US Treasury, visit http://www.treasury.gov.
- For further reading about the banking system, money creation, and various other economic topics, look up the websites, blogs, articles, and books that follow.

## WEBSITES AND BLOGS

- Pragmatic Capitalism, http://www.pragcap.com: Site founded and administered by Cullen Roche, also the founder of Orcam Financial Group, LLC. Especially helpful is the article "Understanding the Modern Monetary System" by Cullen Roche, August 5, 2011, http://pragcap.com/understanding-modern-monetary-system. Also see "Recommended Reading" page (under "Tools & Resources") for listing of publications and articles.
- Monetary Realism, http://www.monetaryrealism.com. Especially helpful is the article "Loans Create Deposits" by

JKH, February 19, 2013, http://monetaryrealism.com/loans-create-deposits-in-context/. Also see "Recommended Readings" tab for listing of publications and articles.

- Understanding the Basics of Banking, http://brown-blog-5.blogspot.com/.

## FURTHER READING ON CHINA'S ECONOMY AND MONETARY STERILIZATION PRACTICES

- "China's Real Monetary Problem," *Wall Street Journal*, September 10, 2010, http://online.wsj.com/articles/SB1000142 4052748703743504575493120916038074.
- "China's Real Sin Is Not 'Currency Manipulation,'" *Economist Online*, September 18, 2010, http://economistonline.muogao.com/2010/09/chinas-real-sin-is-not-currency-manipulation.html.
- "China Faces a Tough Challenge in the Steering of Monetary Policy—The Room for Sterilization is Diminishing," *Research Institute of Economy, Trade & Industry, IAA*, August 23, 2006, http://www.rieti.go.jp/en/china/06082302.html.
- Fan Gang, "China's Monetary Sterilization," *Project Syndicate*, November 29, 2010, https://www.project-syndicate.org/commentary/china-s-monetary-sterilization.
- For frequently updated data regarding China's holdings of US Treasury securities, visit http://www.treasury.gov/ticdata/Publish/mfhhis01.txt.

## ARTICLES ON BANKING AND RELATED ACCOUNTING CONCEPTS

- Ezra Klein, "Yesterdays Tax Revenues Can't Support Tomorrow's America," WonkBlog, *Washington Post*, December 7, 2012, http://www.washingtonpost.com/blogs/wonkblog/wp/2012/12/07/yesterdays-tax-revenues-cant-support-tomorrows-america/.
- AFR Mortgage, "What Role Does Housing and Real Estate Play in the Gross Domestic Product?" *American Financial Resources, Inc.*, November 26, 2012, http://afrmortgage.com/blog/what-role-does-housing-play-in-the-gdp/.
- Kimberly Amadeo, "How Does Real Estate Affect the U.S. Economy?" About.com, http://useconomy.about.com/od/grossdomesticproduct/f/Real_estate_faq.htm.

## OTHER PUBLISHED WORKS

- Paul Sheard, "Repeat After Me: Banks Cannot and Do Not Lend Out Reserves," *Ratings Direct*, Standard & Poor's Rating Services, McGraw-Hill, August 13, 2013, http://ommekeer-nederland.nl/documents/standard-poors-rating-services-lending-creating-deposits.pdf.
- Nicholas Kenaga, "Causes and Implications of the U.S. Housing Crisis," *The Park Place Economist* 20 (1), http://digitalcommons.iwu.edu/parkplace/vol20/iss1/12.
- William F. Hummel, *Money: What It Is, How It Works* (Bloomington, IN: iUniverse, Inc., 2007).

Note: All websites listed were accessed prior to and through the date of publication of this book.

# ENDNOTES

1   "Ezra Pound," Proverbia, http://en.proverbia.net/citasautor.asp?autor=
    15810.

2   Derek Thompson, "Why Economics Is Really Called 'The Dismal
    Science,'" *The Atlantic*, December 17, 2013, http://www.theatlantic.com/
    business/archive/2013/12/why-economics-is-really-called-the-dismal-
    science/282454/.

3   As quoted in "Monetarism," *Wikipedia*, last modified August 25, 2014,
    http://en.wikipedia.org/wiki/Monetarism.

4   Joe Modzelewski, "How a Shoeshine Boy Saved Kennedy Fortune,"
    Etcetera, *The Miami News*, February 20, 1985, http://news.google.com/
    newspapers?nid=2206&dat=19850220&id=2J8mAAAAIBAJ&sjid=
    jwEGAAAAIBAJ&pg=4628,1203198.

5   "Joseph P. Kennedy, Sr.," *Wikipedia*, last modified November 11, 2014,
    http://en.wikipedia.org/wiki/Joseph_P._Kennedy,_Sr.

6   Russell Gold, "Why Peak-Oil Predictions Haven't Come True," *The
    Wall Street Journal*, September 29, 2014, http://online.wsj.com/articles/
    why-peak-oil-predictions-haven-t-come-true-1411937788.

7   Michael D. Bordo, "Gold Standard," *The Concise Encyclopedia of Economics*,
    Library of Economics and Liberty, http://www.econlib.org/library/Enc/
    GoldStandard.html.

8    Wade Slome, "Here's What Warren Buffett Says About Gold and Commodities," *The Cheat Sheet*, March 8, 2011, http://wallstcheatsheet.com/business/economy/heres-what-warren-buffett-says-about-gold-and-commodities.html/.

9    "Ayn Rand Quotes," BrainyQuote, http://www.brainyquote.com/quotes/authors/a/ayn_rand.html.